An Insider's Guide to

SMART
INVESTING

Sun-Jung Choi, CFA, CAIA

ISBN-10:0-9984964-0-5
ISBN-13:978-0-9984964-0-5

First Edition

An Insider's Guide to

SMART
INVESTING

Sun-Jung Choi, CFA, CAIA

DEDICATION

I dedicate this book to you.

I thank you for your curiosity, interest, and aspirations.

ACKNOWLEDGMENTS

My deepest love and appreciation to my family and friends.

I am truly grateful to every single one of you who encouraged me through this journey and shared your thoughts with me.

TABLE OF CONTENTS

CONNECTING THE DOTS BETWEEN INVESTING AND FAMILIAR CONCEPTS

(for that "a-ha" moment of enlightenment)

The main purpose of investing is to achieve increased prosperity. You choose to invest because you desire a higher level of financial security and a general sense of well-being. But what is the point of investing if it creates more fear about your money? Are you tired of worrying about your investments? Has your fear of losing or being wrong or not knowing caused you to behave in a reactionary or emotional way? If so, I'm sure you have some regrets and skepticism because of it — and you're not alone.

Things that Drive Investors Out of the Market

Market uncertainty scares investors away, but uncertainty about investing itself is even scarier. Lack of confidence in the economic structure and lack of trust in an investment industry make people cling to the safety of cash. Being bombarded by the thought of negative outcomes forces investors to prepare for the worst-case scenario, which often pushes them toward inactivity. They hoard cash (or whatever is considered a safe asset) because they perceive investing as "unsafe." And when investors are repeatedly disappointed by unethical practices, they stop investing. Consequently, these practices cripple the true potential and prosperity of both individual wealth and the economic progress of our society.

While investment products have become more sophisticated and regulations have been tightened, the problems associated with investing still exist. Do these phrases sound familiar?

- *"The economy will turn around soon."*
- *"The stock market is expected to outperform in the near future."*
- *"Investors need to stay in for the long haul."*

No one can predict the future of investing. Furthermore, the stock market is a leading indicator of the economy. Thus, it is likely to recover before the economy does. When those positive sentiments from above fail to alleviate investors' frustration, investors remain uncertain and fearful, and their easiest option (unfortunately) is inaction. Not knowing the future market direction is frightening, but not having enough knowledge about investing causes higher levels of fear. Think of it this way: you can bake a delicious cake (sophisticated investment) in a well-equipped kitchen (well-established environment), but what's the point of baking if nobody wants to eat a slice (low participation in investing)?

The prevailing issues in the investment industry are the consequences of actions taken by people *who* invested before and *how* they utilized investing—either for themselves or on behalf of other investors. You've heard the colloquialism, *"Guns don't kill people; people do."* This emphasizes the importance of the user's responsibility and the direct impact of an action. Money enhances our lives when used properly—and so does investing.

Education Eases Tension

In any relationship, including the one between investors and investing, genuine understanding is the key. Misunderstandings can break down communication, and people tend to ignore issues and distance themselves when things don't work out as expected. If you've been unhappy with previous investment experiences, you need to evaluate how you've invested and if you misunderstood some aspect of it. If an investment didn't work out, blaming your adviser might seem to help heal ill feelings, but it does not provide a solution and adds more emotional discomfort in the end.

Education eases the tension that may be inhibiting your investing practices. First, it's important to understand what caused the friction and distrust in order to reconcile what happened in the past. More specifically, you need to understand your own behavior and any problems that arose. What mistakes did you make as an investor? Did you know your risk tolerance when you invested? How did you choose your financial professional? Were you aware of the cost structure in the investment? Were you misled? If so, how can you prevent it from happening again?

Perhaps you're new to investing or have never done it before. The best way to begin is to try to learn more about the process—just like you do at the beginning of a relationship—before making any commitments. It won't work if you jump in unprepared, especially when you feel you should invest but lack the knowledge to do so properly.

Once you understand how investing works, you can become a disciplined long-term investor. The key is to identify your investing priorities in regards to your individual goals and investing method that suits your needs. And in order to know what's right for you, you need to understand the basis of investing. "One size fits all" never works when it comes to investing.

Closing the Knowledge Gap

We often hear things without thoroughly understanding the content. That doesn't mean we didn't pay attention to what was said. It's just that certain types of information are difficult to comprehend initially. Many investors misunderstand investing, regardless of their level of experience. It's hard to detect a misunderstanding on your own, especially when it originates from a lack of knowledge. As the saying goes, "You don't know what you don't know." As a result, investors make mistakes repeatedly without fully understanding the consequences because they don't even realize they're doing things incorrectly.

When I worked as a portfolio analyst, I learned about wealth management/advisory businesses and individual clients/public investors from an analyst's point of view. Working with advisers allowed me to see how they run their practice and interact with clients. I also observed how investors reacted to recommendations and outcomes. I collected data and research from various investment firms (companies that create and sell investment products) and learned how they communicate and work with the *retail* side (advisers/agents/brokers who work with the public) through a *wholesale* network. The concept of "wholesale and retail" is basically the same as in other industries. You can think of the investment company like the manufacturer of the product and wholesalers sell products to retailers, and retailers reach out to end-consumers.

There is a serious knowledge gap among institutional money managers or fund managers, retail advisers, and clients. What makes sense to professionals is not always what makes sense to public investors. Part of the problem stems from the fact that investing concepts are too technical for most of the general public, whereas they may come naturally to financial professionals. Standard deviation and Sharpe ratio might not mean anything to you as a novice investor, which is problematic because you're in a position to accept advice and invest for the sake of preparing for the future.

It's not natural for you to confidently accept market volatility and uncertainty in the long run—especially without adequate knowledge. And seemingly insignificant mistakes are often the result of unrecognized patterns and can greatly impact outcomes.

Learning through Analogies

In the beginning, I had a hard time conveying my points to public investors who didn't have in-depth knowledge about investing. A lot was lost in translation because I used the language of an analyst.

I often felt I was delivering information in a preaching manner, and clients quickly lost interest. In response to this, I started using analogies that people could relate to. Analogies are incorporated not only to enhance a deeper understanding but to help explain why an investor needs to understand (and should not ignore and underestimate) the subject. It helps make technical investing concepts more accessible and memorable by connecting investment terminology with other familiar concepts. It also helps inspire people to learn about investing and engage in the process more dynamically.

Let me explain with an analogy why I wrote this book. Let's say your friends need to get to the airport, and you know how to get there. They are turning left when they should turn right. Wouldn't you want to tell them they need to make a right turn instead? This book is my way of giving you directions and helping you get to your destination based on the roads I've taken before.

Some subjects in this book are related to common mistakes that investors make, and some are recommendations that allow you to retain a higher level of control during the investing process. Experienced investors may relate to some of the subjects I cover more deeply, but individuals who work with financial professionals also will find sections especially tailored to their needs as well.

Intellectual curiosity grows with knowledge, which functions like an enriched fertilizer. If you encounter concepts that you are not familiar with, you would be wise to refer to other sources to accelerate your understanding while reading this book. One thing about knowledge that has proven true for me is that the more you know the more questions you have.

Now, let's begin to connect the dots between investing and what you already know for that "a-ha" moment of enlightenment!

INTRODUCTION— UNDERSTANDING HOW TO INVEST

The unknown is terrifying; fumbling in the dark is aggravating, and unpredictability can trigger emotional discomfort and insecurity. If you don't know how investing works, how can you feel comfortable with it? How can you control your emotions while dealing with constant changes and uncertainty? Many investors seek advice from a financial professional, and yet it's impossible to evaluate somebody else's expertise without a proper understanding of how it works in the first place. For any job that you hire other people to do, you need to know the underlying basics in order to evaluate the quality of their work. Therefore, it's imperative to develop a deeper understanding of the ins and outs of investing—whether you opt to go it alone or work with professionals.

Once you grasp the concepts well enough to apply them in practice, you will become more confident and be better able to figure out the most effective investing method for your personal needs. So, let's get started!

Current Status—What Do You Know about Investing?

If you walked into a giant warehouse or big box store, you would be overwhelmed if you didn't know what to look for or where to find what you wanted. You might find a do-it-yourself tool but feel apprehensive about using it alone. Perhaps you'd discover that the product you intended to buy was too expensive to justify the purchase. You could also find something better than what you originally planned to buy.

Learning about a wide range of investing methods is similar to entering a warehouse. Savvy investors may insist that the best way to invest is "ABC" (which could be any strategy that worked for them), but it may not be the best investment method for you if you are not experienced enough to implement that strategy. Various choices are great, but in the beginning of your journey, you may feel overwhelmed by them, or you might not know where to begin. The best approach is to start the process by acknowledging your current status in terms of your own capability and knowledge about investing.

Self-Diagnosis—What Is Your Investing Level?

If someone asks for your advice on how to invest, how would you answer? Your response to this question is a great way to assess your experience and knowledge level in investing, especially when the question requires specific details about types and methods of investing—not just a definition. Ask yourself a series of relevant questions (as a self-diagnostic tool) when you are unsure about your current status. For example, try answering the following questions:

- What is a mutual fund?
- What is a stock?
- What is a commodity?
- What is an alternative investment?
- What is a robo-adviser?
- What is a fiduciary duty?

Did you struggle to answer any of these? If so, it could be because you don't know the answer or because you know so much that you can't decide where to start. Some investors lack the experience to differentiate between traditional and alternative investments while being familiar with mutual funds and Exchange-Traded Funds (ETFs). You may have had experience in trading commodities but aren't fully aware of more complicated strategies. Do you feel confident about analyzing stocks but not bonds? Maybe you've worked with a financial professional but still don't fully understand the difference between a broker and an investment adviser.

Here's another important question for you—what level of investor are you? You don't need a specific title per se, but you should be able to distinguish if you are a beginner, an expert, or somewhere in between. To make it easy, let's use a scale of 1–10, with 1 being a beginner and 10 being an expert. Where do you fall within that range? You might think you are a 7, but you might actually be a 3. If that's the case, then you've overestimated your level, which may result in an investing method that isn't right for you. If you've failed in investing before, this could be the reason. Perhaps you think you're a 1, so you hired a financial professional. If the experience was unpleasant or left you feeling unsatisfied, it could be related to an inadequate understanding of the importance of the selection process. For the best results, it's vital to determine and acknowledge your investing level honestly. Your game plan for how to invest varies according to your current status.

Game Plan—What Comes Next?

When you deposit money into a bank, you always want to ensure the stability of the institution you use and know how you'll use their services. Similarly, when you put your money into investments, you need to make sure that your investments suit your needs and that you know how to obtain and use different sources of investing to reach your goal. Ask yourself, "What comes next based on what I'm doing?"

After you've answered that one, begin to answer the following questions. Each set relates to a different type of investor, but by answering the questions and reviewing (and updating) your responses on a regular basis, you can familiarize yourself with the process and learn how to figure out what to do next.

If you just started to invest by putting a certain percentage of your paycheck or contribution into an investment account, answer the following questions:

- What types of investments do you have in the account?
- How did you pick them (your own analysis or a recommendation from others)?
- What is the cost structure for each option?
- How often do you review and rebalance your account (change the allocation of your holdings)?

What can you do to improve your current status? If you're having a hard time answering these simple questions, that's a problem that you need to address. It's easy to just go along with investments that seem nice or effortless or are chosen by others—especially when you feel uninformed or overwhelmed, but that's just the type of practice that will harm you in the long run. Knowing what you have is simply a matter of time and effort, not expertise. Whether you chose a specific investment or had someone make the recommendation for you is irrelevant; you have to know the basics of your own investments no matter what. Knowing the basics is not an option; it's a must.

If you believe you have a working knowledge in investing because you know how to trade stocks, bonds, or funds, answer these questions:

- How did you build your portfolio?
- What is the objective of your investment portfolio?
- What is your risk tolerance and time horizon?
- What type of expertise and skill set(s) do you have that relate to your investment strategy?

What can you do to improve your current status? You've had some level of experience in investing, but that doesn't mean you've invested properly. Investors often fall into repetitive routine investing habits for various reasons: comfort level, false judgment, lack of understanding, and so on. Knowing how to trade is different from knowing how to invest.

If you are not investing because you don't know how to, or are taking a break after disappointing results, answer these questions:

- Why are you scared or frustrated with investing?
- Do you think the best bet is to stay out of it because you don't know enough?
- If you decide to keep putting it off, when do you plan to start or resume investing?
- Is it better for you to invest alone or seek advice from a financial professional?

What can you do to improve your current status? Inaction is simple and comfortable, but it's not a solution. The true benefits of investing aren't defined by past experience. It's a causal relationship, and your inaction has a cause. Finding the cause and accepting the reason is the first step toward fixing the issue and moving forward.

If you are working with a financial professional, answer the following:

- How did you choose whom to work with?
- How often do you evaluate your financial professional's work?
- How involved are you in your investment decisions?
- When was the last time you sought a second opinion?

What can you do to improve your current status? Hiring someone to invest money on your behalf doesn't mean you can just forget about investing and let him or her do the work. As an investor, you reserve the right to decide how your money is managed. Working with someone who is kind, or because he or she came highly recommended, is not a reason to believe your money is managed in your best interest. It's important to do your own homework as an investor.

These question-and-answer exercises are oversimplified, but they're a great way to help you easily understand how to build a game plan to move forward, and your answers depend upon your personal situation. It's not surprising that investors who lack the proper understanding of investing have disappointing experiences—and thus become more reluctant to continue investing. If you have no interest or have lost your enthusiasm toward investing, you need to find out why. Like in many other things, procrastination can turn small issues into serious problems. Getting to the heart of the matter right away is your best approach.

No matter what level you are, the starting point is to recognize your current investing level and make an effort to explore other available options to improve your current status.

Time Is Valuable—Why Invest Now?

You work hard and try to save money for the future. The main reason for investing is also to generate income and save money; ultimately, it's for increased prosperity. Investing creates supplementary prosperity. In the past, only people with sufficient disposable income invested, but it has become more relevant to everyone—with increased participation in retirement accounts as well as easy access to trading platforms. More and more people have access to retirement accounts, but they don't use the full capacity because they don't understand how to invest. You might know more than others, but the majority of people simply don't know enough. Consequently, many people view investing as being "too complicated." It's similar to how people feel about math: there are a few students who excel at math, but many are confused and intimidated by the subject.

The simplest answer to "*why invest now?*" is to enhance the value of your money over time (referred to as "time value of money"). The earlier you start investing, the more you get paid for the time the money is invested. Ten thousand dollars in cash today won't be worth the same amount in 10 years because inflation devalues a consumer's purchasing power. In fact, your money's value technically deteriorates if you hold onto cash during an inflationary period. Therefore, sitting on cash *now* means losing purchasing power in the *future*.

Have you ever assembled something, like furniture, by yourself? In the beginning, you probably thought you'd figure out how to do it without reading the instructions. Unfortunately, it may have been more complicated than you initially thought. At that point, you most likely discovered you missed a crucial step and needed to start all over. Such a process is frustrating and even irritating when it happens. Yet, looking on the bright side, it's better to have discovered there is a problem, so you can change your course of action sooner rather than later.

Now, apply that approach to investing. Surely, it's best to discover a mistake in your investing before the problem is magnified. This concept also applies to timing when it comes to investing. If you're not investing *now*, when do you plan to start? Remember, time is valuable.

(Essential) Knowledge + (Customized) Plan = (Long-term) Success

- What's the best way to invest?
- How can you invest wisely?
- What should you do to achieve a satisfying investment result?

The answers are different for everyone. It's like a diet plan designed to achieve and maintain a desirable weight. The best solution differs based on the individual—and you will get the best result when you use a suitable method that works for you. If you have a weakness for sweets, you need to find a way of reducing your sugar consumption. If you tend to eat large meals, your diet plan should focus on strict portion control. Nevertheless, the basic principle stays the same: you cannot eat in an unhealthy way and simply wish to stay fit without regular exercise.

When it comes to investing, the basic principle is to understand how it works. You cannot expect to succeed in investing without necessary knowledge, which is why I've written the following chapters—to enhance your understanding about investing by using analogies that relate to your everyday life.

I want you to be aware of your knowledge level in regard to investing and identify what to learn next. I hope you'll discover what's fundamentally important to you in terms of investing because it is an essential step in becoming a long-term investor. Improvements occur when you recognize your priorities and accept your weaknesses. Once you have a proper understanding of investing, you can figure out how to prioritize and strategize an investment plan that truly works for you.

CHAPTER ONE

GOAL SETTING— WHY ARE YOU TAKING THE TRIP?

If you plan to go on a trip, you do so with a purpose. Depending on your reason, you make different decisions in terms of location, budget, and duration. It also differs based on who you go on a trip with and if you choose to travel on your own or work with a tour guide. The purpose of your trip is the most influential factor in making a functional plan.

Let's think about it further. Is your trip for pleasure, or is it for business? Are you planning to celebrate an anniversary or enjoy a holiday with family (or even Spring Break with friends)? Are you going to attend a conference or advance your education (or perhaps build a relationship with a business partner)? Your plans change dramatically based on the purpose; therefore, the purpose should be specific enough to make a practical plan. Similarly, when it comes to investing, you must specify your primary goal in order to create a suitable approach.

What If All Mission Statements Were the Same?

A mission statement, or Statement of Purpose, is used as a guideline in business. What if the mission statement of all companies was "to succeed" or "to be profitable?" Would they all meet those goals? I doubt it. Similarly, if every investor's goal was "to make money" or "to save and retire," it would be more difficult to accomplish because it didn't include a specified goal and a customized plan.

Detailed goal setting is a prerequisite to building the working plan for your investing needs. After all, you can't succeed if you don't have a clear understanding of your personal investing goals. Your decisions should reflect what you aim to achieve. The best investment choice is the one that has the highest possibility of helping you reach your goal.

Let's revisit the trip analogy. If you thought you could just invest without a plan, imagine taking a trip without knowing why you are going. How are you going to figure out where to go, how much to spend, and how long to stay? Opening an investment account doesn't mean you are ready to invest, nor does it mean you are investing properly. If you own multiple investment accounts, it's prudent to create a main goal for each one as well as all of them in total. The money you choose to invest was earned through hard work. Treat it cautiously by taking the necessary steps; your investment plan should start with goal setting and strategic planning—not chasing after returns and numbers.

Making the Right Plan

Investors often set goals that are too general and thus destine the plan to failure. What is your goal in investing? Why and how are you investing in this particular account? Broad answers such as, "It's for retirement" or "It's for college" don't yield enough information. If the goal is for retirement, when do you plan to retire? What is your time horizon and liquidity need? What kind of lifestyle do you want to maintain after retiring? An investor should answer these specific questions as a way of establishing both the goal and the ways in which to achieve it.

Let's take an employer-sponsored savings plan as an example. Your reasons for participating in this account are not the same as your co-workers' reasons. Hence, if you have the same portfolio as others in the plan, you are likely not paying enough attention to your investment choices or have made unintended mistakes. If you haven't saved enough for an emergency fund, building up your personal savings is probably more important than making contributions to a retirement account. While one of your co-workers may have a goal to pay off his or her student loans, you might be better off taking full advantage of an employer-matching contribution benefit or maximizing your tax deferral first. If you are closer to the retirement age, you may want to prepare for the next stage of your *life cycle* (by making more conservative choices), whereas retirement may not be an immediate concern for others (so they may make more aggressive investment decisions). Remember, each investor's goal varies in relation to his or her personal situation and priorities.

Need a Tour Guide?

We all have travel preferences. Some people enjoy having the freedom to travel on their own schedule, while others prefer following the advice of a tour guide. There are benefits and drawbacks associated with each, and it all depends on the main purpose of the trip. Occasionally, though, we have to do things differently despite our preferences.

Let's say you typically prefer traveling without a guide. If you're heading somewhere you've never been, and you do not speak the local language, a tour guide is essential. And if you're embarking on the trip of a lifetime, you'll probably want a local tour guide to show you around the spots you might otherwise miss. You might also opt for some extra help just for the sake of being efficient with your time.

This decision should be based on what's most important to you (i.e., your priority), as well as what you're looking for (i.e., your goal). Deciding whether to work with a financial professional is the same. Your personal situation determines the suitability of the action plan in how to invest.

Learn to Recognize Your Limitations

It's also important to acknowledge and accept your own limitations. Think of how this relates to your accommodations as well. Just because you want to stay in five-star hotels doesn't mean you can afford to do so. In terms of travel, you may not like having a tour guide, but certain destinations can simply be too dangerous for you to explore on your own. In terms of investing, even though you are reluctant to pay for an advisory service, investing alone without necessary expertise can be detrimental. If you don't have an emergency fund or disposable income, you cannot afford to invest—yet. Therefore, building up your savings or reducing debt should be your immediate priority. It's critical to be realistic and select the best option that helps you achieve your long-term goals while also recognizing your limitations.

Making the Choice to Go It Alone or Ask for Help

Once you've isolated your goal and made a plan, it's time to figure out how to implement it. For example, you have a working knowledge of investing, but one of your accounts consists of inheritance money that requires a high level of expertise. You may choose to work with a financial professional only for that particular account. Maybe you've been working with someone regularly, but choose to work on your own for a small individual account through an online trading platform. You may choose to work with multiple professionals with different levels of expertise as well. There is no one right or wrong answer that applies to everyone. Therefore, it's important to compare available options to find the best action plan for your investing.

If you've never invested before, it's wise to work with a financial professional who can offer you appropriate guidance. He or she can assist you with goal setting and strategic planning. But how do you select the right person? This topic is covered in detail in later chapters, **Chapter Thirteen** through **Chapter Seventeen**.

When you hire a travel agency, the agent needs to understand your personal situation to plan the trip on your behalf. If the agent tells you not to worry about a thing and promises to plan "the best trip" without getting to know you, you should view this as a huge red flag. Such an action should tell you it's nothing but a sales pitch. On a similar note, how can anyone build a portfolio for you without a full understanding of your goals and priorities?

A sophisticated investor notices these types of red flags early on. Remember, it's your responsibility to maintain control of your own money and take the necessary steps to ensure a financial professional has your best interests in mind.

Parting Thoughts

There are plenty of choices and flexibility when it comes to investing. Be sure to figure your capabilities and honest limitations into every investment decision—and study potential benefits and risks associated with available courses of action. You can't create a realistic plan without getting into detail, so be especially attentive to setting goals and choose your action plan wisely.

Goal Setting: Establish your investing goal in detail and select a practical action plan accordingly. Proper goal setting is a prerequisite to building a functioning plan.

CHAPTER TWO

RISK TOLERANCE—
HOW SPICY DO YOU
WANT YOUR FOOD?

Risk is an easy term to understand if you think of it in terms of spice. For example, when choosing a salsa at a Mexican restaurant, your choice is based on your tolerance for different levels of heat (i.e., mild, moderate, hot, and ultra-hot). When investing, you do something similar. You choose your risk tolerance level to make sure that your investment portfolio suits you. It's critical to pay attention to the level of risk you *can* and *are willing to take* in regard to your investments (by the way, ability and willingness are two very distinct things). It's imperative that you recognize and accept your true risk tolerance level without allowing yourself to make choices based on your emotions at a given time. This is the only way to build a prudent investment portfolio.

Ability Does Not Equal Willingness

Risk tolerance is one of the factors that you take into consideration when determining how aggressive your portfolio should be. There's an old phrase that says, "Just because you can do something doesn't mean that you should." This also applies to investing. Just because you're capable of taking risks doesn't mean that you should or are actually willing to do so. Likewise, a willingness to take greater risks doesn't mean you can afford to.

For example, if you have the ability to take a risk right now, a financial professional is more likely to educate you about ways to enhance your returns by taking on that higher risk. He or she should also explain why your objective should remain at a certain level. In this case, your ability to take a risk is enough to justify the aggressive objective, but your willingness to do this might not be enough. Investors can become lost when financial professionals already have a pre-set plan, or if they don't realize the outcome of an investment decision. Consequently, the portfolio may be too volatile for them to handle, which is one of the main reasons why people don't stay in investing through downturn markets and end up selling low. Unfortunately, investors often don't realize how risk averse they are until they lose money.

Control the Heat

Here's an important question to consider: Should you have a more aggressive portfolio just because you can, or should you take a more conservative approach because you're concerned about volatility and prefer stability? When you seek advice from a financial professional, you expect guidance and assistance. Naturally, you're more likely to accept recommendations and less likely to speak your mind if you believe it's best to follow a given direction.

If you don't want to deal with higher risk and volatility, you don't have to. Don't let others make that decision for you. After all, the consequences are ultimately yours to deal with. Would you let others decide how spicy your food should be? The cook cannot force you to eat spicier food because he or she thinks it tastes better that way. If you just accept the recommended spice level, you might discover that it's too spicy for your liking and wind up feeling sick afterward. You don't have to take risks that you're not comfortable with. Voice your thoughts directly in terms of the desired risk level you're at ease with regarding your investments. It is a financial professional's duty to lead investors in the right direction based on their profiles; it is an investor's responsibility to recognize proper risk tolerance for investments.

The Downside of Being More Willing Than Able

Some investors are happy to take higher risks although they cannot afford to do so. In this case, their willingness exceeds their ability. Think of it this way: you enjoy spicy food although your body cannot handle the consequences. When investors take risks that are greater than their actual ability, it's often because they don't understand what's at stake, or they ignore embedded risks involved with investment choices.

Some investors are overly confident, and it can be challenging to change their opinions. Sadly, some financial professionals may simply let investors have their own way, allowing them to take unsuitably risky positions as long as their orders are placed as *unsolicited*, which relieves them of responsibility. From a financial professional's perspective, it would be somewhat uncomfortable and difficult to say no to a client request. For some, it's easier to give in than to deal with an "unreasonable" request or advise him or her that the investment is simply too risky to consider. No matter what the situation, financial professionals need to be up to the ethical challenge of educating investors who want to take an improper level of risk. They are the investors who need enlightenment and education in order to be guided properly.

What's Your Portfolio Called?

Investment portfolios are constructed with different risk/return profiles and objectives. The most conservative portfolio's objective is often called *Capital Preservation*; and as the objective moves gradually toward being more aggressive, it is called *Income*; *Growth with Income*; *Growth*; and *Aggressive Growth* or *Speculative*.

In order to define which objective is suitable for you, your personal information is collected and categorized by a financial professional into various predetermined levels. Typically, this document is called an Investment Policy Statement (IPS), and it's used as a guideline to target an appropriate level of aggressiveness with respect to your portfolio's construction and investment objectives. For example, if you're near or at retirement, then you may be looking to maintain the money you have while maintaining minimal risk. Therefore, your objective falls under the designation of *Capital Preservation*.

To use another analogy, when you work with a financial professional, you can think of this IPS as cruise control. With an IPS, you limit how your money should be managed by stating your risk/return profile and objective. To do this effectively, you need to express your view on how a financial professional will drive your car (or manage your money). If you are not willing to take risks, your money manager shouldn't take unsuitable risks on your behalf. If you want to withdraw your money anytime you want, you shouldn't invest in products with a long-term time horizon or lockup period. At the same time, setting your cruise control to a slower speed means you'll achieve slower results. Likewise, if you are risk averse and have a designated *Income* objective, it's unrealistic to expect higher returns than those achieved in a *Growth* portfolio. The speed level you choose for the cruise control is similar to the aggressiveness of your portfolio: slow and steady or fast and furious (but not a mixture of both). Keep in mind that it's your car (money), and you are the one who determines what speed (level of aggressiveness) is acceptable.

You Are the Money Manager

When you cook your own meal, you can decide how spicy to make it. However, that doesn't mean you should ignore your tolerance level. You still need to acknowledge the amount of spiciness your body can take as well as how spicy specific ingredients are. When you invest by yourself, you have full control of your investment decisions and need to know your risk tolerance level based on both your ability and willingness to take risks.

When people invest alone, they often end up with scattered investment holdings due to excessive usage of the *bottom-up approach*. In cases like these, investors focus on an individual investment opportunity before (or without) looking at the overall economy or sector outlook. And if you trade whenever you come across attractive investment opportunities, you can easily lose sight of your portfolio's big picture and end up owning risky investments that don't match your comfort level. It's important to recognize your risk tolerance level and build your portfolio accordingly.

Trade-Off Between Risk and Return

When it comes to making an investment decision, a sensible choice is to seek a higher return per unit of risk or a lower risk per unit of return. Confused? Let me clarify. It makes sense to take a risk when the expected return is higher than the associated risk (i.e., return enhancement standpoint). Also, it's logical to accept a lesser return if the associated risk is lower than the expected return (i.e., risk management standpoint). For instance, a 5% expected return with an expected risk of 5% is better than a 5% expected return with 10% expected risk. However, if the latter helps diversify your portfolio significantly (by generating income or protecting you from inflation), then that could be a better option for you. Once again, "One size fits all" doesn't work in investing.

Nevertheless, it's imperative to remember that higher expected returns are directly linked to higher expected risks. More importantly, your desired risk/return profile should be evaluated on both upside and downside perspectives. Higher risks have more upside potential— but at the same time, more downside risk as well. If your investments have a lower risk level, you may have less room for growth but greater downside protection.

Another useful approach is to consider the total risk in your portfolio in comparison with your holdings as it should be in accordance with the aggressiveness of your investments as a whole. In other words, taking a greater risk means owning more volatile investments and thus having a more aggressive portfolio. If you take a higher risk to target a higher expected return, your investment holdings contain riskier assets; thus, the overall portfolio is more aggressive and volatile (i.e., spicy). On the other hand, if you are willing to accept a lower return because of your reluctance for higher volatility, the portfolio should reflect less risky investments and be relatively conservative (i.e., mild).

The bottom line is that everything should flow in one direction when you look at your risk level, expected return, and the aggressiveness of the portfolio. If it doesn't, it's a good indicator that your portfolio doesn't take your real risk tolerance into consideration, suggesting it's time to rebalance your portfolio.

There's No Harm in Reevaluating Your Preferences

I like spicy food, but if it's too hot for what my body can handle, I cry when I eat and suffer afterward. For this reason, I've adjusted my order on occasion after a server reminded me of how spicy the dish was. Likewise, in terms of your risk tolerance, you must deal with the consequences of making the wrong choice when you invest. You may be tempted to do what you want (such as bearing an unsuitable risk even if you don't have the ability to do so). You may even rationalize your decision by being overly optimistic about expected returns or justify underestimating the associated risks. You probably don't want someone to tell you that you can't afford to do what you want because, after all, it's your money. But before getting defensive, try to accept the guidance objectively. It's wiser to yield to reasonable advice than to remain rigid and have regrets later. For more detail, see **Appendix B, Review as Q&A**.

Fear (Emotion with Risk) and Greed (Emotion with Return)

We all want to grow our investments, but none of us want to lose money. Sounds simple enough, but this doesn't really determine proper risk tolerance level. However, it conveys an important message about the most common emotions related to investing: greed and fear.

Investors often focus on one side of the risk/return profile, not fully realizing the consequences. As a result, risk-focused fear and return-focused greed often cloud an investor's judgment regardless of his or her expertise or knowledge level. If you want a higher return, you need to take a greater risk; whereas if you want a lower risk, you should be willing to accept a lower return.

Remember, your portfolio needs to flow in the same direction in terms of risk level, expected return, and aggressiveness regardless of how it's built. Otherwise, the portfolio is likely to be unbalanced and unsuitable in the long run.

Parting Thoughts

To succeed in investing, an investment portfolio must be suitable for you. And to do this, you need to identify your goals and risk tolerance. If you were wrong about your risk tolerance level in the past, your portfolio probably had an inappropriate approach. Be realistic with your comfort level and assess your risk tolerance accurately, and you will be able to invest more effectively.

Risk Tolerance: Acknowledge your suitable risk tolerance level in terms of both ability and willingness to take a risk respectively. You don't have to take risks you're not comfortable with just because you can (ability). Correspondingly, you shouldn't take a risk that is beyond your ability simply because you want to (willingness).

CHAPTER THREE

INVESTING CAPABILITY— HOW MUCH WEIGHT CAN YOU LIFT?

When you work out, you should know how much weight you can lift to avoid hurting yourself. Similarly, investors need to acknowledge and accept their true capability in terms of both expertise and time. Don't mistake years of trading experience for expertise, and don't confuse what you're asked to do with what you're capable of doing. When you accept your true capability, an investment decision can be more efficient and disciplined.

Investing, Not Gambling

Unsuitable risk-taking behaviors often come from a misunderstanding of risk tolerance levels as discussed in **Chapter Two**, but also result from a misunderstanding of investing capability. If an investor doesn't have sufficient knowledge but still makes money in investing, is it really a result of his or her skills? Or is it luck? If that's what you're looking for (good luck), there is nothing wrong with that. However, the problem arises when investing is treated like gambling (without appropriate acknowledgment).

One of the major differences between investing and gambling is the willingness to lose. People gamble with the expectation of having a chance to win "big," so they are willing to lose for the possibility of winning at some point at the expense of permanent loss of capital. People invest with the expectation of growing money, but many investors are reluctant to lose (referred to as "loss aversion"). Therefore, investing shouldn't rely on luck, and yet an investor's overestimation of his or her own investing capability is similar to depending on good luck. Naturally, an investor expects the (unrealistically) optimistic outcome, undermines associated risks, and ends up with a bad investing experience.

We often edit our memories, consciously and unconsciously, to feel better about ourselves. It's easy to recall proud moments and leave out the truth when it comes to our own abilities and talents. It's easier to pat ourselves on the back when things go well and point fingers at others when things don't go as planned. Many investors love to talk about how much money they've made from investing. They make it sound simple and doable, but before you jump in, you need to face your capability honestly.

It's tempting to view the past with a selective memory, but that can cause more harm than good. Acknowledging (and accepting) your investing capability is critical because it is directly connected with investment decisions. Don't bite off more than you can chew if you want to benefit from investing.

Uncontrollable Factors

Have you ever felt lucky with uninterrupted green traffic signals or frustrated having red traffic signals one after another while driving? It's just a coincidental timing of signal changes or affected by how other cars around you drive, but it influences your mood as well as the actual progress to the destination. On a similar note, an investor experiences both overconfidence and discouragement stemming from these uncontrollable factors.

Unexpected acquisition news on a stock could make the price go up dramatically, or a sudden natural mishap could change the value of a certain *asset class*. Glorifying a positive result often affects an investor's following decisions negatively when it leads to misjudging the investing capability. Also, disappointment from a negative outcome brings about discouragement and lower confidence in investing itself, which can inhibit someone from being a long-term investor. Be careful not to pat yourself on the back or blame yourself for the investing outcome that you didn't have control of. The final outcome, rather than the cause, stimulates and accelerates our emotions more vigorously. It's important to understand the reason for an outcome in order to invest with discipline and objectivity.

Recognition of Your Loss Aversion

Loss aversion is our reluctance to lose and is more relevant than risk aversion in investing. More specifically, an investor's risk-taking behavior is closely linked to reluctance (and unwillingness) to lose money rather than overall risk tolerance or volatility level. Investors are willing to take risks when an expected return makes sense to them but still don't want to lose their money nonetheless. Some can handle short-term losses more than others, but people won't invest if they believe there is a possibility of losing all of their money in the end. Long-term investors stay in investing, regardless of a current gain-and-loss situation, as they expect investments to grow eventually.

The recognition of your loss aversion can give you a reality check of your own investing capability. A statistical term, Value at Risk (VaR), measures the financial risk by breaking it down into three components: the probability of loss, estimated amount of loss, and specific time frame. Looking into the breakdown of components makes understanding and measuring of loss aversion easier.

- How much volatility (total risk) or downside risk is too much for you?
- What's the likelihood of the threshold loss you are not willing to bear?
- How long can you be patient dealing with volatility or loss?

Remember, it's not just about generating a return; there is always a trade-off between risk and return. If you misunderstand your investing capability, you end up taking risks that you don't even realize that you are exposed to.

The Truth Hurts Less in the Long Run

Online trading tools are easy to use, but that doesn't mean it's easy to invest or that you're ready to do so. Ask yourself this question: "Are you sure you can analyze all the investment products and strategies by yourself?" Perhaps you've been trading stocks for a while. "Can you analyze individual bonds or *derivatives* as well?" Maybe you've worked in an advisory business for a long time, succeeded, and built a reputation. "Do you still have enough time and resources to do everything alone even after your business has grown to a different level?"

This is a sensitive subject because it may hurt your pride (and bruise your ego) to admit the fact that you cannot do something. If others watch you working out at a gym, you may be reluctant to admit you can't lift heavier weights; but if you don't use the proper weight, you can end up injuring yourself. The whole reason you exercise is for better health and strength. What's the point of working out if you get hurt in the process?

It's not easy to accept when a third party reviews your investments and tells you what you've been doing is wrong. It's tough to take criticism and admit your mistakes. Sometimes, the truth hurts, but long-term positive outcomes always outweigh short-term pain when you accept your true capability. If you misjudge your capability, you run the risk of reducing the potential benefits you could've otherwise had when investing.

Parting Thoughts

The most dangerous investors are those who believe they know something when they actually don't. Accepting your capability will help you make prudent investment choices. It will also reveal your limitations and constraints. And you can always take the necessary steps to transcend your current situation, which will bring you greater rewards in the long run.

Investing Capability: Accept your investing capability honestly and do not confuse the impact of uncontrollable factors with your ability. Feeling confident about your investing capability is different from overestimating or misunderstanding what you can do.

CHAPTER FOUR

INVESTMENT EVALUATION— WHAT DO YOU THINK OF THIS YELLOW CHAIR?

A beautiful yellow chair stands in the middle of the store. If someone asks me what I think about the chair, I'd say, "It's pretty." This doesn't mean I want to buy the chair or that I would recommend others buy it. It doesn't matter how lovely the chair is if it doesn't go well with the rest of the other furniture in your home. Similarly, an investment can be attractive, yet that doesn't mean it will fit into your portfolio. Investment evaluation starts with looking at your existing portfolio and incorporating an investment opportunity that would maximize benefits for the entire portfolio.

Investment Opinion vs. Investment Decision

The herd mentality makes investors gravitate toward things that others invest in without fully recognizing or accepting the risk involved. This is a term you may already know: FOMO, or fear of missing out. When this happens, people often think they're making a decision, but they're really just jumping on board with what others are doing.

As an analyst, I've been asked my opinions about various investment topics, and I remind people that an investment opinion is different from an investment decision. Statements like the following are all too familiar:

- *"This stock is a famous money manager's pick."*
- *"A hedge fund manager, who made an incredible return last year, is very bullish in this sector."*
- *"There is a rumor that this company's drug will get regulatory approval soon."*

- *"That legendary strategist was on TV last night stating this asset has stable market value and an inflation-hedging benefit."*
- *"What do you think about this stock with a new model coming out soon?"*
- *"I've heard this is a place to put money right now."*

When these types of statements entail the subsequent question of "should I invest in this?" my initial response has always remained the same: "What do you have in your portfolio?" Of course, I can express my opinion on a subject, but not when it comes to how it might affect an investment decision. General opinions shouldn't be translated into investment decisions without further consideration from a portfolio perspective.

Unless I know what you've had for breakfast or lunch, how can I suggest what kind of food would be the best for your dinner? On a similar note, unless I know what you have in your portfolio, how can I suggest which investment is suitable for you?

I've researched a wide range of investments as a portfolio analyst. Although I've agreed that an investment would work great given the market condition, I've never used it in a particular portfolio if it wasn't the right fit for *that* portfolio. In that case, the final decision had little to do with how great the investment was; it was simply unsuitable for the total portfolio.

If you have a room full of red furniture, the yellow chair might look rather silly no matter how pretty it looked on its own in the store. It might fit perfectly in your house, but it might also ruin the harmony and flow if you already had several others. Your current portfolio is the first thing you need to consider when evaluating an individual investment. Remember to make investment decisions from a portfolio perspective, not on a stand-alone basis.

There Is Always Another Next Big Thing

Eventful news and trends stimulate the interests of investors. It's exciting to converse and exchange investing ideas, especially when it's about how to make money. When you stay in investing long enough, you'll eventually discover an investment opportunity that you feel is too good to pass up. However, nothing's ever too good to pass up if the investment is unsuitable for you to begin with.

For example, imagine discovering a stock that interests you. As you've already gravitated toward it, you start to pay more attention to its price movement. And the more you follow it, the more convinced you are that it's a remarkable buying opportunity. Now, you're all fired up with the stock's upside potential and have a strong urge to buy (i.e., all in the name of being "too good to pass up"). This is when you need to pause. Why? Because this is greed talking ... especially if you haven't done solid research from the standpoint of the total portfolio as a whole. Don't rush into a financial decision simply because you're afraid you'll lose the *next big thing* if you don't buy in. Trust me, there is always another *next big thing*.

You need to find out if it fits with the rest of your portfolio before jumping into an investment opportunity. Remember the yellow chair? The more you look at it, the more you want to buy it. But before making an impulse purchase, you need to examine how it will fit in your house. Where are you going to put it? How many do you need? Is there another piece of furniture that suits your home better?

Like most investors, you probably wonder if there's room for speculation in an investment portfolio, meaning you want to invest in something that would be riskier than your long-term strategy. Going back to the previous example, if you're motivated by speculation, you'd buy the stock because you're willing to take on additional risk for that particular investment. This is equivalent to buying that yellow chair regardless of how it would fit in your house. So, in short, there is room for speculation.

The key point to remember is that the capacity for speculation depends on an investor's risk tolerance and ability to recognize such a speculative choice as a risk-taking behavior. It becomes problematic when an investor thinks of this speculative behavior as a core investment decision due to lack of knowledge. Core investment decisions (long-term perspective) shouldn't be compromised by taking speculative actions (short-term perspective).

Understanding the Proper Investment Decision-Making Process

One day I got a phone call from an investor. A particular stock went public the same day. I'd sensed from his tone that he was excited about the stock and wanted to buy it immediately. He asked my opinion. He emphasized that he was well-informed about the stock-related news, and many of his "smart" friends were buying it. After reviewing his entire portfolio, the recommendation was to pass on the stock; he took my advice.

A couple of months later I ran into him, and he thanked me for talking him out of buying the stock. Its price had fallen dramatically. I told him that I'd expect the same reaction from him even if the stock price went up because we made the investment decision from the portfolio's perspective, not just based on the stock valuation. The Initial Public Offering (IPO) stock was unsuitable for his portfolio, regardless of the expected return, in relation to the risk to his total portfolio.

Imagine if my response were, "You're welcome. I told you so. I knew it would go down." What if the stock went up, and an investor blamed the financial professional for the missed opportunity of making money on the stock? This happens more often than you'd think.

The first response of the financial professional stems from an ego-driven mentality. The second reaction of an investor results from a misunderstanding of the proper investment decision-making process. When you seek advice about an investment opportunity with the intention to buy in, you probably already feel like you've discovered the *next big thing*. To overcome that emotion, you need to learn how and why a recommendation has been determined. Even though it's simply a curiosity-driven question, investors need to understand that an investment opinion is different from an investment decision. Otherwise, they are inclined to react to the outcome with heightened emotions, which eventually leads to short-term and irrational behavior.

It's imperative to take account of your current portfolio, as well as your future plan, in order to evaluate and position investments during the ongoing research process. Remember that the yellow chair can be pretty but still look bad in *your* home.

"Buy" for Him Could Mean "Sell" for Her

An investment can have a *sell* recommendation for one person while having a *buy* recommendation for another. Similarly, a strategy that works well for you can be harmful to someone else. This may sound odd, but it's true when you look at it from the perspective of the total portfolio, not based solely on the strength of an individual investment.

For example, imagine reading an article in a renowned investing publication that ABC stock has upgrade consensus with a *buy* recommendation. It's a technology stock with strong cash flows and consistent growth, and, yet, this stock isn't a *buy* for you if your current portfolio already has too much exposure to the technology sector. Even if you intend to buy stocks in this sector, ABC stock may not be the best choice if stronger alternatives exist. You might be better off investing in an international equity fund rather than this individual stock if your total portfolio will benefit from a higher level of diversification.

Now, let's say you own ABC stock. Leading positive news on the stock doesn't mean you should hold it in anticipation of a potential value increase. It would be more beneficial for you to sell when the stock price is high enough if the stock has been too volatile for your risk tolerance level. You also need to remember that there are tax consequences associated with gains and losses. So, although an investment may be a wise *buy* for someone else, it can still be a *sell* for you.

Parting Thoughts

It's important to make investment decisions by considering how harmonious that choice is in relation to your current portfolio and personal circumstances. Imagine how messy your house would be if you bought every piece of furniture just because it seemed pretty. Be cautious, especially when a good (or seemingly good) investment opportunity presents itself; it can be good for others, but that doesn't mean it's good for you.

Investment Evaluation: Analyze each individual investment by taking your existing holdings into consideration from the total portfolio's perspective. Your current portfolio and personal situation define what's right for you regardless of the attractiveness of an investment.

CHAPTER FIVE

INVESTMENTS WITH EMOTIONAL TIES— DO YOU LIKE IT BECAUSE YOU ARE FAMILIAR WITH IT OR BECAUSE IT IS REALLY GOOD?

Assuming all the ingredients and prices are equal, we are more likely to choose brand name products over generic brands because the brand name offers recognition value. We feel comfortable with things with which we are familiar, and that feeling of comfort creates loyalty and trust in value. When it comes to an investment analysis, it's critical not to confuse familiarity or comfort level with the true value of an investment.

Unconditional Rationalization

Having a preference for investments that you are familiar with is perfectly fine (referred to as "buy-what-you-know strategy"). What makes it unsuitable is the unconditional rationalization that stems from familiarity. If an investment has financial strength and offers attractive *intrinsic value* on top of familiarity, it's beneficial to an overall portfolio. Nonetheless, a problem arises when our own familiarity selectively filters the information we receive. When this happens during analysis, any *material* changes become irrelevant because we're too busy rationalizing what's taking place.

Perhaps you own a particular investment simply because it is what it is (not based on the research of what it can offer). Retail investors pay more attention to stocks just because they are more familiar with stocks than other investment products, such as bonds or *derivatives*.

Investment decisions based on familiarity lead to overvaluing "what we know," which makes us more emotionally attached to those investments. You can invest in what you are familiar with, but you also need to remain receptive to new information and other available options.

Difference Between Familiarity and True Knowledge

Because of familiarity, we often feel we know more than we actually do, and an investment seems more attractive than it actually is. Familiarity makes our investment decisions emotional as we feel personally attached to them.

Often, investors pursue stock in companies they've heard of or seen (or whose products they've bought). If you use a certain brand of detergent, drink a well-known soda brand, or drive a specific car, then the related company stock may appear to be an attractive investment. Living in Las Vegas, I've come across many investors with interests in casino and gaming stocks. Also, many people like to own their employer's stock even long after they retire. They may not be aware of the company's financial strength or intrinsic value, but they're comfortable enough with holding the stock because they are familiar with it. As they put more trust in the company they worked for, they choose to keep the stock without further research. This tendency results from a comfort level based on familiarity.

Let's say you have a family member who works at XYZ company. XYZ stock may seem more accessible as you feel somehow related to it on a personal level. If that family member celebrates a promotion and shares how fast the company has been expanding, you'd start developing positive biases toward the company and ignore the fact that there are other stocks with similar news that are even better values. You'd feel more comfortable with it than with some random option. However, that familiarity could also give you a false impression, which leads to irrational investment decisions based on subjective judgment. It's important to recognize that feelings of self-assurance stem from emotion-based familiarity and must be considered as such when determining the financial strength of an investment.

Understanding What Soft Value Means

Sometimes, people invest because they want to support a specific cause. This is not a result of emotion. A good example is *socially responsible investing (SRI)* or *impact investing*. It is guided by the desire to make a positive impact on society and express value through investing. This investment strategy supports good deeds and social contributions and doesn't simply focus on financial returns by either avoiding investments that do not provide a social benefit (aka negative screening) or buying investments that reflect social responsibility (aka positive screening).

These types of investments have personal value that is more meaningful than numbers; in these instances, investing is not just about maximizing profit. Often, gifted and inherited investments are categorized as emotionally attached investments that are unproductive and speculative. It's fair to criticize this approach when the personal value becomes too extreme, but it's important to acknowledge the soft value of the investment as well. Although it may not be the best investment in terms of financial return, what matters the most is how satisfying the final outcome is to the investor. Personal value and moral beliefs have intangible value and are more deeply satisfying than just the bottom line, which is known as the soft value of an investment.

Another way to think of the soft value is to consider the non-financial value of art. The joy of owning something you cherish could exceed its appraisal value, and the soft value is equally meaningful and shouldn't be ignored. When an investment has personal value, or represents a moral belief you support, the valuation method should also include its soft value in lieu of financial return. Unless it's completely unsuitable for you in every way, you can consider it a solid investment decision.

But keep in mind that it's even more crucial to evaluate such holdings on a regular basis to determine if they're overweighed or if their fundamentals have deteriorated. After all, it's essential to remain impartial when investing.

Parting Thoughts

Familiarity gives us an authentic sense of comfort and an accordingly skewed perception of actual value. When familiarity is a factor, it is critical to evaluate all the possible negativities and costs that could far outweigh benefits with an investment. It's also crucial to avoid emotionally attached investments and recognize that it's different from acknowledging the soft value of an investment.

Investments with Emotional Ties: Do not confuse familiarity with the true value of an investment. When a positive bias due to familiarity turns into an unconditional rationalization, any information will be immediately filtered via a biased view (jeopardizing objectivity). It's also important to understand the difference between an emotionally attached investment (need to avoid) and the soft value of an investment (need to accept).

CHAPTER SIX

PORTFOLIO CONSTRUCTION— DO YOU WANT BOILING WATER OR ICE WATER?

Imagine having only boiling water or ice water. We may need boiling water to cook something but prefer hot water for a cup of tea. Perhaps you like water at room temperature by the bed during the night, and you may enjoy cold water but not necessarily ice water due to tooth sensitivity. To lead a normal life, we need water in a variety of temperature ranges, and that diversity applies to investments as well. The investment universe has a wide range of options from which to choose, so take advantage of all the different return/risk levels of investment opportunities that exist between the *extremes*.

Avoiding the Bipolar Portfolio

Simply put, investors build their portfolios by owning investments that support their long-term goals. Often, investors see where opportunities exist based on two components: one for growth and one for income (or safety). Therefore, their portfolios end up with two extreme ends and nothing in the middle. This sometimes happens because people believe that the extremes offer the best value (referred to as "barbell strategy"). However, this "bipolar" portfolio comes with negative consequences when it results from the investor's lack of knowledge about available investments.

At retail stores, products are usually displayed by categories, such as size, color, or brand. Think of investment products in the same way. Investments can be categorized into different groups as well. Stocks can be divided by the size of the company, which is called *market capitaliza-tion* and ranks from mega-, large-, mid-, small-, or even micro-cap. And bonds can be categorized by credit rating or the type of issuer.

As an example, a portfolio might consist of 50% in small-cap stocks and 50% in *high-quality bonds*, which are two extreme ends. To remedy these extremes, an investor could have 30% in large-cap stocks, 20% in *preferred stocks* or *convertible bonds*, 20% in *high-yield bonds*, and 30% in high-quality bonds. Just because you want to participate in equities does not mean you must stay in all types or one specific type of stocks. In this example, by reducing common stock exposure only to large-cap equity, we have lowered the overall risk level associated with these stocks, given the small-cap equity's higher volatility. Accordingly, this investor can now afford to take additional risks in bonds or alternatives that lie between the *extremes* because the risk level in equity has gone down.

This works the other way around as well. Having a positive view on equity doesn't mean you should increase the overall allocation to it. You can keep the same allocation percentage but invest in riskier categories with higher expected returns. You can choose to invest in a certain category that's considered to be safer or riskier within the scope of the same *asset class*.

A portfolio is also "bipolar" if it has only a small number of stocks. If you have a handful of stocks, and they represent half of your total portfolio, your risk factors are too concentrated as price movement of those hold-ings can affect your entire portfolio dramatically. You are well advised to pay close attention to the percentage, not just the dollar amount, of each holding from the portfolio's perspective. Generally speaking, small-sized accounts have fewer holdings than larger accounts due to high transaction costs or minimum investment requirements, etc. Investing in diversified funds is also a great way to solve this issue and ensure proper diversification in a relatively small-sized account.

You can also end up with a "bipolar" portfolio if half of your wealth is invested but the rest is sitting in cash. If this is the case, it's best to change the portfolio's objective to be more conservative while increasing the total investment dollar amount. And if all you know are the *extremes*, and you've invested alone until now, it's time to consider working with a financial professional who can assist you in finding superior opportunities that exist in between them.

As emphasized throughout this book, you need to recognize what you can bear in terms of associated risk as well as how you can maximize your opportunities by building a portfolio with investments that best suit your needs. You don't have to adjust your risk tolerance or limit the investment universe; you can adjust the portfolio according to your desired risk level.

Think of portfolio construction as the execution of an investment strategy. And there's a vast universe of investments/investment strategies that can benefit you.

Balancing Defensive Growth and Aggressive Income

Imagine lining up all your investments on a horizontal line starting from the most aggressive to the most conservative. What would you put as first, middle, and last? How would you display your portfolio holdings on the horizontal line? This is a simple practice to self-diagnose if you have too many extreme-end investments.

Now imagine you are putting each holding on a scale to achieve the right balance for your portfolio. Let's say your target risk level is 50, given 0 is no risk at all and 100 is the maximum risk. You don't need to try to achieve 50 by putting 100 and 0 (or even 90 and 10) on two extreme ends. You can target the same goal by organizing your investments at different intervals in between the *extremes*. Once you've done this, you can see if there are other opportunities you can take advantage of in the middle of the line which result in the same expected outcome.

Let's revisit the previous example with 50% in small-cap stocks and 50% in high-quality bonds. The earlier example was changed to reflect an allocation of 30% in large-cap stocks, 20% in preferred stock or convertible bonds, 20% in high-yield bonds, and 30% in high-quality bonds. With the new allocation, growth components (stocks) become more conservative with larger capitalization and income generation; income components (bonds) become riskier with a mix of high-yield bonds with a lower credit rating. Your growth component becomes *defensive* if you invest in large-cap stocks rather than small-cap stocks. And your income component becomes *aggressive* if you invest in high-yield bonds rather than high-quality bonds. Sometimes, *defensive* growth can be safer than *aggressive* income.

Defensive growth is a way of conservatively participating in growth components, instead of distancing yourself from them because of their associated high volatility. *Aggressive* income is a way of collecting income but not losing upside potential in growth components because of an income-driven preference. Think of it as mixing boiling water with ice water. You can invest in growth *defensively* as well as in income *aggressively*.

Parting Thoughts

If you explore and use all the available investment opportunities, you can manage your portfolio more efficiently. It's prudent to target a lower risk level for the same expected return or a higher expected return with the same level of risk-taking, which can be achieved by using different types of investments.

Portfolio Construction: Broaden your investment options by researching what exists between the
extremes of growth and income (or safety). A variety
of investments with different characteristics exist, and
the utilization of all the different levels brings about
higher efficiency in investing.

CHAPTER SEVEN

PORTFOLIO REVIEW— DOES THAT UGLY TREE STILL LOOK BAD WHEN YOU STAND ON THE TOP OF THE MOUNTAIN?

Have you ever noticed how the view changes depending on your proximity to something? For example, an ugly-looking tree doesn't look nearly as bad when you're on top of the mountain instead of standing next to it in the forest. Similarly, when you review existing holdings in your portfolio, you should take a broad view. Stay focused on the big picture of the total portfolio without worrying about each holding's individual value or daily price fluctuation.

Obsessing Is Shortsighted

Reviewing investments regularly is necessary to evaluate your progress. However, checking price movements every day or paying excessive attention to an individual holding will leave you feeling anxious and tense. Getting hung up on small and insignificant data points often leads to emotional reactions and misjudgments.

Imagine being a farmer. After planting seeds, a small range of plowed dirt is all you can see. Even if you're convinced that your crops should be growing faster, continuously checking on their progress won't make them mature sooner. The maturation process takes time. It's natural to think that giving them more water or fertilizer will speed things up; however, it may actually do more harm than good. Checking your investments excessively can also harm your portfolio, as you sweat over trivial details and make rushed decisions with momentary emotions.

In the field of *behavioral finance*, research shows that investors make irrational decisions based on analysis with a narrow perspective, like what happens when you stand too close to something and can't see all the details (referred to as "narrow framing bias"). It's important to take a step back to see the big picture and make objective assessments. The main goal of a portfolio review is to make sure your investments are on the right path from a total portfolio perspective.

Playing Favorites Can Hurt You

When you have multiple holdings in a portfolio, it's easy to be more optimistic or pessimistic about some of them. Naturally, the performance of those individual holdings has an impact on you. Why? Because you have likes and dislikes across many positions, which means you are biased during the review process. When your emotions are involved, it's difficult to see the big picture; as a result, your analysis is no longer objective or rational.

Let's assume your favorite holding's value fell unexpectedly. You might consider buying more, because its current price is low, and downplay the fact that your exposure to the holding could be improperly overweighed by an additional purchase. Conversely, if the price of a lesser favorite went down, you'd feel like you'd made a foolish choice in buying it and be upset. Doubt would set in, and you would want to sell immediately.

When it comes to an individual investment, there is no ultimate answer for the best recommendation unless you see the big picture. Favoritism is emotionally driven, and investment decisions shouldn't be emotional decisions. Review and evaluate individual holdings from the total portfolio's point of view. By disciplining yourself, you'll make more rational decisions.

Your Reaction Can Reveal Your Suitability

As an investor, it's helpful to identify which investments evoke dramatic reactions. If an investment triggers too much intensity and anxiety, then it's a good indicator that it's unsuitable for you. There are lots of reasons for this: too much volatility or exposure, lack of liquidity, or just the type of investment itself.

Remember when I asked in **Chapter Two**, "How spicy do you want your food?" It's important to acknowledge your risk tolerance level in terms of both willingness and ability to take risk. If an investment elicits strong emotions, the holding is too risky for you to own in the first place, which can reveal your willingness to take risks. Listening to your attitude and gut instincts are constructive ways of finding out if an investment is suitable for your portfolio.

Parting Thoughts

A portfolio review is as important as portfolio construction; it is a part of the ongoing investment decision-making process. Listen to your attitude as an investor, but be careful not to overanalyze and magnify shortsighted issues—which is what we do when we lose sight of the big picture. The key is to maintain control of the right balance from the portfolio perspective as a whole.

Portfolio Review: Focus on the big picture of your overall portfolio during the review process, so you avoid making emotional decisions. Investment decisions shouldn't be based on spontaneous reactions or trivial details.

CHAPTER EIGHT

STRATEGY AND IMPLEMENTATION— IS IT REALLY GOOD FOR YOU IF YOU CONSUME THAT MUCH?

Healthy or otherwise, consuming too much food (or even too many vitamin supplements) isn't good for you. As a general rule, too much is always worse than too little. As an investor, you may come across an investment product or strategy that sounds so attractive that you feel certain about its benefits, but you need to be wary of excess. Investors often succumb to their passionate convictions and extreme optimism, and this results in unbalanced exposure in their portfolios.

Conviction or Obsession?

Determination is hard to change. Once you've formed a strong opinion, it's difficult to adapt to a new viewpoint. While learning about investing, it's easy to be captivated by a specific investment idea. Investors sometimes latch onto investment strategies, feeling certain that those choices provide the "best" way to invest and grow wealth. Unfortunately, strong convictions can easily turn into obsessions if you're not careful.

This isn't a matter of a portfolio's lack of diversification because the portfolio was intentionally built that way. When an investor makes up his or her mind in a very concrete way, even the research process is compromised. Objectivity and judgment go out the window, and other alternatives are frequently dismissed despite their ability to enhance the portfolio as a whole. If this happens to you, you may underreact to new information and overuse your investment strategy or product (referred to as "choice-supportive bias").

Having passionate convictions is productive when investing because it means you have discovered what works for you. What makes it destructive is excessive usage and a mind that is closed off to other alternatives (similar to the unconditional rationalization mentioned in **Chapter Five**). The investment universe continues to evolve and grow on a constant basis, so try not to conclude that your choice of investing is the "best" way. Too much *good stuff* can turn into *bad stuff*.

Lost Opportunities Can Cost You

The right investments are beneficial if used properly, but excessive usage could harm your portfolio. If you let your conviction override your logic, you may fail to find better opportunities in other areas. Opportunity costs are lost prospects that you could have had elsewhere. Every decision you make, including an investment decision, has an opportunity cost (which is different from the direct consequences associated with that choice).

For example, Investment A may have a return of 5% while Investment B has a negative return of 7%. Imagine choosing Investment B. The direct consequence of that choice is a loss of 7%, but the opportunity cost would have meant a gain of 5% if you invested in A instead of B.

Low-cost investment products, such as *passively managed index funds*, are advantageous to investment portfolios—but that doesn't mean your portfolio will benefit from owning these products exclusively (for more detail, see **Appendix C—Glossary**). Sometimes, it's worthwhile to pay the extra fee for specialized skills and take advantage of active management. When you first learn about *technical analysis*, it may sound intriguing. But if all you see is the graph and that solidifies your decision (because the chart says so), you can run into trouble.

We always have opportunity costs when we make a decision. If you're ignoring other opportunities because of your obsession, the opportunity cost is too high. In fact, you could see a better outcome by being less myopic. Do not magnify the benefits by rationalizing potential pitfalls simply because you feel sure of something. It's critical to assess all embedded risks, including opportunity costs.

Break Your Investment Habits

Everyone has habits that result from staying in their comfort zone. You might keep going in one way of investing just because you have gotten into the habit of doing things a certain way. The enormity of the investment universe can feel overwhelming, so people often use the same method of investing as a way to create a sense of control. If this sounds familiar, or if you find yourself consuming too much in one domain, you should consider educating yourself further or seeking guidance from a financial professional.

If you're stuck in a pattern of investing just because of your comfort level, your opportunity costs will be too high to deal with in the long run. Break your pattern and be transformed into something more positive by accepting differences and learning alternative solutions to making strategic investment decisions.

Parting Thoughts

It's impossible to conduct objective and thorough research when you're too occupied with a preconceived idea. But take heart—you don't have to start from scratch after abandoning the investing method that has worked for you for so long. Just be cautious not to use it excessively or become close-minded and blinded by your own convictions.

Strategy and Implementation: Do not let your passionate conviction interfere with your objectivity. Strong beliefs are valuable as long as they don't lead to excessive usage and a mind adverse to alternatives. You can maximize the benefits of your choices with balanced judgment and usage.

CHAPTER NINE

RESEARCH—
ARE YOU SURE IT'S A FACT?

Imagine running into an old friend. She's wearing a ring and tells you, "I love diamond rings." Do you assume that her diamond is real? Remember, "I love diamond rings" and "I'm wearing a genuine diamond" are completely different statements. The first is an opinion, while the latter is a fact. Investment research involves collecting both facts and opinions, but you should be able to differentiate between them.

Learn to Interpret the Intention Behind an Opinion

Investors often find themselves overwhelmed during the research process as there is far more information than they need. Various opinions can be helpful, but it's important not to be swayed by opinions regardless of whether or not the given information is intentionally misleading.

Many investors use a search engine's financial sites to obtain investment-related information. This is free and easy to access. It provides a variety of data, such as price movement, graphs, and other relevant information (including news, trends, and opinions). Be sure to separate opinions from facts and try to determine when opinions are based on valid and reliable facts (with transparency).

Opinions, specifically, beget drama as a way to grab your attention. Most people prefer to read articles filled with opinions because they have more pizzazz. And let's face it, facts can be dry and boring. But people with opinions have intentions. Some want an audience to learn or agree with them. Others are looking to establish their reputation and credibility. And many people just want to share their views.

Identifying the intentions of an opinion-maker is an effective tool to use when filtering information. Everyone has opinions, but not all of them are based on solid information.

Don't Confuse Presentation with Proficiency

Flashy presentations with fancy words can be impressive, and they are often confused with proficiency. Skilled salespeople are charismatic and know how to steer conversations to achieve their personal goals. But if their opinions are laced with deceptive intentions, your money could be in jeopardy.

When money is involved, there will always be opportunists who try to skirt around the main issue and work in their own best interest. If you've ever been on the receiving end of a demanding sales pitch, then you probably felt like you were being forced to make a decision. People with honest intentions don't pressure others, so if your adviser is pressuring you, it's a red flag. If you aren't ready to make a decision, don't.

When you go to an electronics store, a sales representative may help you find what you're looking for, and he or she won't pretend to be an engineer or technician. Unfortunately, that's not always the case in the investment industry. People with sales skills often pretend to be investment experts, even if they don't have that specific expertise. They tend to make big claims and emphasize what investors want to hear, such as reassuring them of the benefits associated with a specific investment, like high returns, safety, guarantees, and so on.

Some salespeople really seem to believe in what they sell. Either that or they're just great pretenders. Train yourself to focus on the quality of the content—not just the perceived expertise of the salesperson. Ultimately, your final decision should be based on sound research. It's critical to validate information that you receive in order to look beyond what's presented to you. If something sounds too good to be true, it usually is.

Opinions with Facts Are Still Just Opinions

An opinion can be just as it seems, or it can be based on a fact. For instance, saying "I like oranges" is a simple opinion; however, saying "I like oranges because they are a good source of vitamin C" is a fact-based opinion. When an opinion is based on a fact, it's more important to distinguish it from a fact-less one. Here's an example: "I like this investment" is a fact-less opinion whereas "I like this investment because it has been paying a consistent dividend" is an opinion based on a fact. When you encounter a fact-based opinion, you should validate the truthfulness of any facts associated with it. To be precise, fact checking must be a part of your research process, and you need to analyze both the fact and the opinion respectively.

Many investors follow knowledgeable expert opinions, which are typically based on facts. When we agree on an issue with others, we make an instant connection and form an even stronger opinion. However, a problem arises when a positive impression overrides our judgment, making it difficult to identify a fact because we are so drawn to the opinion. Honestly, this is one of the hardest things for me to overcome during the research process. So, I've developed a habit of asking myself constantly if what I'm reading or hearing is a fact or an opinion as well as checking the source of the information. As readers or listeners, the veracity of the information is up to us to discern, so remain aware that investment opinions from intellectually savvy professionals are also just opinions.

Avoiding Cherry Picking (aka Taking Things out of Context)

Sometimes, trends trigger your urge to invest (as discussed in **Chapter Four**). A recommendation for something that sounds familiar or is popular with investors can lead you to want to invest without having a full understanding of the investment. Imagine that a highly reputed expert said, "Buying at a weakness on ABC and XYZ stock presents an attractive opportunity in a current news-driven market." What part of that sentence stood out to you? If you're like most people, ABC and XYZ stocks were probably the most memorable. But what about the rest of the recommendation? When specific names are mentioned, those names stand out more than the overall meaning, and that can be highly problematic without the full content.

Before considering those individual stocks, you must understand the meaning of the entire context. What's a news-driven market? This occurs when news and headlines affect market direction prominently. What does buying at weakness mean? It means the price level has dropped from its fair value. Do you know what the underlying strategy is? In this case, it's "value investing," which is a type of investing style (for more detail, see **Appendix B, Review as Comparisons**). What industry/sector/style do ABC and XYZ stock belong to? You'd need to research that to find out. Remember, it's imperative to take the full content into consideration during the research and evaluation process.

Once you decide that a strategy is relevant and beneficial, the next step is to evaluate how the investment fits into your portfolio. By acknowledging the portfolio's objective, as well as your existing holdings, you can review whether or not "value investing" works for you in terms of risk level and diversification. You may not need (or be able to afford) to participate in "value investing" given your suitability. If there is no room to begin with, it's a waste of time to research further on those individual stocks. On the other hand, the strategy itself could work, but your portfolio might already have a large exposure to the same sector with ABC and XYZ stock. Therefore, purchasing additional stocks could unbalance your portfolio. In that case, it's better for you to explore different value stocks instead.

Sadly, we all have selective hearing. If you've already established an opinion about something, you'll be more inclined to accept other opinions that can confirm your own (referred to as "confirmation bias").

Good news about an existing holding gives you relief and satisfaction. When it confirms something you already believe, you are more likely to overweigh that good news and underweigh the bad.

When an investor doesn't know enough, he or she filters the information in a way that's not intended. The original recommendation is insightful, but, due to improper cherry picking, it may be implemented in a way that could conclude with an investor owning an unsuitable investment. Taking things out of context can turn the medicine into poison.

Parting Thoughts

As an investor, you must analyze facts instead of looking for opinions that reassure you about your choices. The purpose of investment research is neither to prove your point nor to find advocates. Be receptive to valuable recommendations, but reserve judgment until you assess all relevant information.

Research: Distinguish a fact from an opinion during the research process. A smart researcher is receptive to various recommendations but knows how to assess the grounds of an opinion and the reliability of a fact.

CHAPTER TEN

VALUATION— HOW MANY ITEMS DID YOU BUY JUST BECAUSE THEY WERE ON SALE?

Imagine shopping during the holiday season. The price of two items is exactly the same, but one has a 50% off sales tag while the other is not on sale. You would assume it's a good deal to buy the one on sale. Like most people, you would probably think that the quality of the sale priced item was better because its regular price is higher than the other one. And yet, what if the sale item was just overpriced to begin with? In reality, the retailer probably has excess inventory due to the original over-pricing, which leads to price discounting. This also happens to investment products. Without its fair value, nobody can tell the value of the discount. Don't invest in something just because you think you're getting a good deal as it's cheaper than before.

When a Good Deal Isn't Good for You

Have you ever paid attention to how much you spent instead of how much you saved on sale items? Sales and discounts encourage people to buy things impulsively and to buy more than what they need. Sellers offer discounts as a marketing tool to attract customers. From the seller's perspective, it is a profitable transaction if a larger quantity is sold even if the profit margin becomes narrower with a discount. On the other hand, buyers only get a good deal if they get what they need at a discounted price.

Many investors are attracted to the "discounted" investment even though it doesn't fit into their portfolios. What makes it worse is that people are drawn to investments that are only seemingly discounted, not truly discounted. In this case, investors tend to underestimate the associated risk as they are overly excited about the idea of getting a good deal or misled by the sellers. Various marketing tactics make consumers believe it's a good deal.

An investment is considered to be either *cheap* or *expensive* in comparison to its fair value (commonly calculated by using a *relative valuation method*). It's also described as *trading at a discount or premium*. An undervalued investment is attractive because it has a higher potential for price appreciation if the value adjusts to its fair value. But it becomes problematic when investors focus solely on how inexpensive it has become from the past price level rather than comparing it with its fair value. If you don't know the fair value, how can you tell if it's *cheap* at the current price? It doesn't matter how much the price has gone down if the initial price was overvalued in the first place. You shouldn't assume you're getting a good deal only because it's a lot cheaper than the past price. First, you need to find out if the original price was the fair value or not. For more detail, see **Appendix B, Review as Formulas.**

Identifying the fair value is a prerequisite before measuring the discount value. Begin by investigating *why* an investment has become *cheap* instead of chasing a "discounted" investment. Getting a good deal only works if the deal is truly undervalued and worthwhile for your portfolio. Otherwise, it would cost you more than the initially perceived discount given the high opportunity cost. In other words, you spent more than you saved, and the savings was not worth it.

Learn and Apply the Principles of Cost-Benefit Analysis

If an organic product costs more than triple the price of a non-organic one, you'd be reluctant to pay that price, wouldn't you? Yet, you may consider buying it if the price difference is reasonable given its additional benefit. Simply put, it's sensible to buy something if the benefits exceed the involved costs; these are the basics of *cost-benefit analysis.*

Understanding the cost structure is extremely important in an investment analysis. It doesn't matter how great the investment opportunity is if that "greatness" is eroded by an unreasonably high cost. An investment may appear attractive on the surface, but if it costs too much, its potential benefit is already reduced. Thus, the investment becomes unattractive after taking its cost structure into consideration. Conversely, an investment that seems just average at first may turn out to be a good buying opportunity because its cost-efficient feature provides additional benefits to the overall value.

For instance, when you buy 2,000 shares of a non-traded investment product or private placement at $10 per share, your investment value may show up on your statement as $20,000—but this doesn't accurately reflect the true value of the investment if the fee is already embedded into the product price. And when the product is illiquid, you'd be penalized if you chose to liquidate earlier than the committed period. This type of information is disclosed in the prospectus, but the technical wording may put off investors, leaving them with only a cursory understanding of the details. Unfortunately, from an investor's viewpoint, taking the seller's explanation seems easier.

High-cost products are not entirely bad. They only become problematic when investors don't fully understand the investment's cost structure and limitations (or when they don't recognize the potential consequences that apply given their personal circumstances). Investors with near-term liquidity needs shouldn't invest in something with redemption constraints, such as long-term lockup periods or early redemption penalties. Some products become trendy even though they impose an unreasonably high fee because they provide (or seem like they do) relatively stable market values or features that are catered to lessening an investor's fear. But investors who are fee-sensitive shouldn't invest in high-commission products. For more detail, see **Appendix B, Review as Formulas**.

Many investors are aware of the importance of cost structure but do not fully understand how to properly conduct a cost-benefit analysis. You don't have to know how to calculate Net Present Value (NPV) or read an entire prospectus line by line to determine a proper cost-benefit analysis. Realistically speaking, the internet is one of the most time-efficient tools for general investors. You may have to sift through a lot of information, but you should take advantage of the resources available to you. If you are not sure which information to follow or where to search, check out regulatory websites, such as the Financial Industry Regulatory Authority (FINRA). Simply look for the category titled "**For Investor**," and you'll find reliable, independent information (for more detail, see **Appendix D—Resources**). Refer to other available sources and seek a second opinion, if needed. Your time and effort will be well spent.

In the end, nobody can work in your best interest better than you. Don't assume that an investment recommendation is valid (i.e., benefits outweigh costs) simply because you think you're well-informed or because you like your financial professional. Take extra steps to find out if the investment is beneficial. It doesn't take much time and effort, but it will make a huge difference in regards to the outcome.

No Such Thing as a Free Lunch

Some companies offer gift cards or free meals to people who attend seminars or visit their businesses. They say you don't have to buy or commit to anything; all they ask you for is your time. One thing these companies have in common is that what they sell usually requires a long-term commitment from you. Most likely, the company's profit margin is high enough to recoup the marketing cost they spent for your time. That's how they're able to offer free incentives, even if only a few people buy into the deal.

Investment-related seminars work the same way. Not all of them are after your wallet, but be aware of the offers you receive for free. The given information is more likely to be what a buyer/investor wants to hear, not a full disclosure of the facts. Therefore, it's tempting to believe it's a good deal. Even if seminars provide useful information, an investment decision shouldn't be made with only a fraction of the given information. Impulse buys are, by definition, unplanned, and investment decisions should always be planned.

A scarcity premium is only justifiable when something is truly scarce, but a wrongly perceived idea of scarcity often leads us to make imprudent decisions and think we are getting a good deal even when we are not. Consumers are often tempted by phrases like, "Only one item left in our inventory" or "the sale ends this Sunday." Odds are that there are more products coming in soon, and another sale will happen in the future. Don't take the bait. Many investment schemes lure victims into their deals this way. Remember, investment decisions come with consequences, more so than other purchases.

Parting Thoughts

Everything has value, and we all want to maximize our *bang for the buck*. The discovery of an investment's fair value is required to detect any mispricing for the purpose of investment valuation (i.e., to determine if it's undervalued or overvalued). Furthermore, it's imperative to take the cost structure into consideration to maximize the value that can be derived from an investment.

Valuation: Do not choose an investment simply because it's discounted. The fair value must be determined in order to measure the accurate discount value, given its cost structure. Investment decisions shouldn't be made based on incomplete information that is presented to you as a good deal.

CHAPTER ELEVEN

INVESTMENT DECISION— DID YOU THINK HE WAS FEMALE BECAUSE OF HIS NAME?

A name can tell you many things, such as nationality, sex, and even religion (sometimes). Have you ever made the wrong assumption based on someone's name? Perhaps you thought a man was a woman because of the name. Or maybe you mistook someone's nationality based on a common last name. That could easily happen. Usually, it's not a major issue until it brings about a negative outcome, such as in an interview or a business meeting. When it comes to investing, it is a big deal every single time it happens. Do not guess about the strategy of the investment based on its name.

Know Your Investments

Because many investment products exist, investors often take the name as a summary of the investment for the sake of time efficiency. However, the name can't possibly summarize a complicated investment strategy— and it becomes more problematic when investors misunderstand the content because of its name.

Surprisingly, many people pick their investments based on the name especially when it comes to retirement plans. Some are not even fully aware of what they own. Choosing five different funds by the name alone and allocating 20% into each one is neither a suitable investment portfolio construction nor diversification.

Before buying a car or a major appliance, you probably check consumer reviews or compare product descriptions. With a similar degree of effort, you can find valuable information about investment products. Visit relevant company websites, use search engines, or seek advice from others to learn more. It's too risky to choose an investment by the title.

A Name Is a Sales Tool

Investment companies compete to sell their products just like any other entity; therefore, their product names have to be appealing (or simple) enough to catch investors' attention. Newly created investments as well as existing products gain popularity due to market demand (either actual or perceived).

For instance, alternative investments are investments that are not traditional, such as stocks or bonds. Due to the complexity and extreme diversity associated with alternative investments, they are mainly used (or should be used) by large institutional investors or accredited investors (for more detail, see **Appendix D—Resources**). They include a wide range of products, and people have different opinions about what alternative investments are or which products are categorized as alternative investments. From the standpoint of research and analysis, commodities or *managed futures* are alternative investments. However, in a retail financial service industry, they are not considered as alternative investments when they are offered through mutual funds mainly because they are liquid. Most illiquid investments, such as non-traded investment products or private placements, are categorized into "alternative" investments in a retail financial service industry, and the term "illiquid" seems to be replaced with "alternative."

One of the distinctive characteristics of alternative investments is illiquidity, but illiquidity does not mean "alternative." Honey is sweet, but not all sweets are made out of (or called) honey; alternative investments are illiquid, but not all illiquid investments are alternative investments or provide benefits of alternative investments. And yet the term, alternative, is so broadly used that retail investors often misunderstand the strategy and nature of "alternative" investments. More specifically, they may agree to invest in "alternative" investments for their diversification benefits and/or income potential, but may not be aware of the *illiquidity risk*, lack of transparency, or embedded cost that comes with those investments.

While high competition among suppliers (i.e., manufacturers) incentivizes sellers (i.e., wholesalers and/or retailers) with high commissions, it also attracts investors with enticing phrasing, such as low volatility or zero-floor concept. Remember, the name of a product is also a sales tool; just because something sounds good doesn't mean it is good.

What the Name Doesn't Tell You

Just like you can't tell the characteristics of a person by name only, you can't fully understand an investment by its name only. Take funds, for example. Funds are categorized into different objectives based on the profiles stated in the prospectus. Let's say there are three different funds under the name of Moderate Asset Allocation. The first asset allocation fund contains various types of investments, including commodities and *preferred stocks*. The second asset allocation fund consists of individual stocks and bonds. The third one is a *fund of funds* that invests in multiple funds. If you want to add diversification benefits to your current holdings of stocks and bonds, the first one is better for you as it contains different *asset classes*. If your account is relatively small, the second or third fund is better than the first one because it helps build a diversified portfolio without requiring you to own multiple holdings. Yet, if you are fee-sensitive, you may not like two layers of fees coming from the fund of funds; as such, the second fund is the best option for you. Each fund's strategy is unique even though they are under the same category (with similar titles).

Money market funds are often misunderstood as well. I've met investors who mistook them for cash because of the name; needless to say, they were surprised with their negative value. The funds invest in short-term debts, such as commercial papers, repurchase agreements, bank acceptances, and U.S. Treasury bills. Therefore, if the value of those holdings goes down, investors should anticipate negative value. These funds can also end up with a negative value after the associated fees are deducted, such as operating expenses; although, the value changes are relatively inconsequential. Money market funds aim to invest in securities with minimal credit risk, not zero risk. Thus, they're not the same as cash. For more detail, see **Appendix D—Resources**.

Insurance products with similar names have different investment options from which to choose and different restrictions. They also have a wide range of expenses, liquidity schedules, turnover rates, capital gain carry forwards, penalties for early redemption, and so on.

The same mutual fund offers several share classes with different fee structures. Generally speaking, an "A share" is a front-load fee mutual fund, while a "C share" usually carries a back-end fee. Why would you pay a higher fee if it has a *no-load mutual fund* share class? Depending on how the distribution and management fees are charged, the fund may have multiple share classes such as a "T share," a "P share," or an "R share." One fund may require a minimum investment amount or charge a redemption fee while others do not. Some funds are offered as no-transaction-fee funds, but they come with a minimum holding period, and an investor will pay a transaction fee only if he or she sells them within a restricted time frame.

Even though the name of the fund represents its strategy fairly well, other factors can still influence the fund's characteristics. For instance, imagine a fund called XYZ Large Cap Growth. After a dramatic downturn in an equity market, *growth* stocks become more like *value* stocks (for more detail, see **Appendix B, Review as Comparisons**).

In this case, the fund's strategy has stayed the same, but the market environment made a difference. Hence, the outcome will differ from what you originally planned if you were to target *growth* style investing (referred to as "unintended style drift").

Let's look further into other funds. An index fund is created by tracking a certain index, such as Standard & Poor's (S&P) 500 or Dow Jones Industrial Average (DJIA), thereby replicating the performance of the underlying index. An index fund can fully imitate the index performance (broad market exposure) or be narrowly focused (sector or credit rating). A sector-specific fund can be an index-based fund or an actively managed fund. If an investor is fee-sensitive, an index-based fund is a better choice than an actively managed fund. An international bond fund can either hedge or un-hedge its currency risk. So, if you want to minimize currency risk, you need to make sure your international bond has a currency risk-hedging ability. Unconstrained bond funds are called "unconstrained" because the restriction is limited so that strategies vary widely. Some funds have flexibility to *short*, meaning to target profiting from prices going down, while others with the same name are restricted from doing so. You can invest in managed futures through multi-CTA (*Commodity Trading Adviser*) mutual funds, but they have different transparency levels in terms of allocation and track record. Also, some funds are taxed as a partnership, so investors have different tax consequences to consider. Therefore, you should know all the *material* facts about the investment given your personal situation. For more detail, see **Appendix C—Glossary**.

Parting Thoughts

Innovative and sophisticated investments continue to be introduced into the market. It's simply impossible to convey the investment content solely through the name. Evaluate all the material information before choosing your investments because the name can't tell you what you need to know in order to make a suitable investment decision.

Investment Decision: Do not make an assumption about the content of the investment based on its name. If you do, you can easily misidentify the strategy and unintentionally end up with an investment that is unsuitable for you.

CHAPTER TWELVE

DIVERSIFICATION— CAN YOU MAKE A DELICIOUS SOUP WITH ONLY CHICKEN AND NOODLES?

How much do you know about cooking? You may not know a lot, but I bet you can answer this question. Do you think you can make a delicious bowl of soup using only chicken and noodles? If someone hands you only two or three ingredients to make the soup, it's unfair to criticize the end result for lacking flavor. You'd want all the ingredients, right? Spices. Vegetables. Now, think of making your investment portfolio more "delicious" through proper diversification.

Diversification Equals Balance

In theory, diversification means investing in different investments with a low correlation to one another. A correlation indicates how one investment's value fluctuates in comparison to another. Assets with negative correlations move in different directions, while those with a positive correlation move the same way. A high or low correlation also indicates the degree of movement for each one. Therefore, if your portfolio is well diversified, it prevents all of your holdings from moving in one direction to a similar extent. As a result, it reduces the total risk in your portfolio; more specifically, it reduces unsystematic risk, and thus decreases total risk. For more detail, see **Appendix B, Review as Comparisons.**

Looking at diversification benefits from a different angle, doesn't it make sense to take advantage of all the products and strategies out there to build the most effective portfolio? It's like making that soup. You'll do better by using all the ingredients you need rather than limiting yourself to just a few. And what if you need to fix a mistake or your preference changes? If you've made it too spicy, you can fix it by adding more broth. If you've used too many noodles, you can take some out to enhance the flavor. And if you discover a fresher chicken, you might want to replace the current one. When you don't have (or use) other options, the result is less than optimal.

Still, some investors don't believe that diversification has a significant impact, but it actually reduces total risk in a portfolio. At the same time, you're simply missing out on opportunities if you don't take advantage of various investment products and strategies. Diversification is effective risk management and thus enhances your risk-adjusted return.

Invest in Needs Not Wants

Want is different from need. Just because what you want is available to you doesn't mean you should (or can) use it. Proper diversification levels differ depending on an investor's priorities and how to achieve it is also based on each investor's capability, including their level of risk tolerance and objective.

For instance, if you prefer sufficient liquidity in your portfolio, it's unsuitable to own an investment with a long-term time horizon or a lockup period restriction. In this case, the associated *illiquidity risk* is too high to justify the possible diversification benefits. If you can't afford to participate in *private equity* or *managed futures*, it's not what you need to begin with. It doesn't matter what kind of diversification benefits it could add.

If you don't know enough about a certain strategy, you are better off staying away from it and seeking an alternative solution. If you don't know how to analyze individual stocks and bonds (or if your portfolio size is too small), it's wise to focus on researching funds that include those individual holdings so that you can rely on the fund manager's money management skills.

As always, be realistic and try not to fixate on things that are out of reach. You can still build a diversified portfolio within your scope. If it turns out to be insufficient, you can work to increase your capability or seek advice from a financial professional to achieve your desired level of diversification. What makes it right for you includes whether or not it is feasible for you to achieve.

Strategize Your Target Diversification

The incremental benefits of diversification tend to diminish when more investments are added to a portfolio. And during distressed times, the benefits associated with diversification may change, especially when everything moves in a similar direction. Moreover, personal situations change how much value can be derived from diversification.

Many investors claim to understand this concept, but their portfolios often reveal something totally different. Owning a large number of holdings doesn't mean that you've achieved diversification. It's not the case if over-diversification erodes the benefits (referred to as "diseconomies of scale"). Having positions with a low correlation to one another also doesn't mean your portfolio has proper diversification. The performance will suffer if associated costs are too high to justify the value. If the investment is out of your capability, it's unsuitable for your portfolio nonetheless. Without the appropriate target diversification level, your portfolio could just end up being a diversification-want-to-be. It's equally important to acknowledge your target diversification in the same way you establish the investment objective.

Where Can I Get It?

When you work with financial professionals, you should keep in mind that they have different ranges of products and strategies they can offer to clients, depending on their affiliated firm's operational capability as well as their own expertise.

For instance, a financial adviser's main business is selling insurance products. Naturally, he or she would put more emphasis on pros than cons in insurance products to you. If you want to participate in *derivatives*, this adviser may discourage you from doing so, not because it's unsuitable for you but because he or she can't trade them.

Additionally, different firms have diverse restrictions and guidelines on illiquid or high-commission products. If an adviser belongs to a Broker/Dealer firm with strict restrictions on following Financial Industry Regulatory Authority (FINRA)'s suitability rule, he or she has to follow the company policy, thus offering a higher level of interest alignment with clients by ensuring whether or not the product is suitable for them. For more detail, see **Appendix D—Resources**.

When selecting a financial professional, you should be given everything you're looking for from a diversification point of view. If not, it's time to find someone else to guide you. It's vital to understand not only the person's ability to give advice to you but the background of the brokerage firm or custodian (or clearing house), its company policies, and the rules that can affect the scope of investments they offer.

Parting Thoughts

You can maximize the benefits of all your investment opportunities through proper diversification. The types of investments you can own rests not only within your capability, but in the financial professional whom you choose to work with as well.

Diversification: Explore and take advantage of all the investment opportunities within the scope of your capability (or your financial professional's capability). Proper diversification helps produce positive outcomes while reducing the total risk in a portfolio.

CHAPTER THIRTEEN

SELECTION AND EXPECTATION— WOULD YOU EXPECT TO GET THE BEST CHINESE DISH AT AN ITALIAN RESTAURANT?

If you went to an Italian restaurant, you wouldn't expect to get the best Chinese food. As such, it's unreasonable to complain about the quality of a Chinese dish at an Italian restaurant. You can't fault the cook. He or she could have made you an amazing meal, but you can't get upset if you ordered something that the restaurant doesn't specialize in. This is a simple case of unrealistic expectations. You have to take responsibility for the choices you make, and you can't be upset when you expect someone to be able to make every type of cuisine flawlessly.

The same rule applies when working with financial professionals. These individuals possess diverse expertise and work with the public through different systems. It's important to select the right person to handle your needs and to expect realistic outcomes.

Know Who You Work With

A wide range of financial professionals work with public investors. What they do and what they are capable of varies widely. They hold different licenses and certifications; hence, each has a different level of expertise and capability. In the case of financial advisers, the title is defined so broadly that it often confuses people. The following section illustrates this diversity. I don't want you to be overwhelmed with the acronyms and industry terminology, but be aware that all these individuals can call themselves financial advisers.

- An Investment Adviser Representative (IAR) renders fee-based financial advice as a fiduciary and works for a Registered Investment Adviser (RIA), which can be a hybrid model by being additionally registered with a Broker/Dealer (B/D) for commission-based transactions.
- A Registered Representative (RR) transacts (recommends) investment products usually for a commission and works at a B/D firm; follows FINRA's suitability rule, but this may change based on the implementation of the Department of Labor (DOL)'s fiduciary rule. For more detail, see **Appendix D—Resources**.
- A dually registered adviser works at both a B/D and B/D's corporate RIA channel as a RR for commission-based transactions and an IAR for fee-based transactions.
- A retirement plan adviser assists companies and plan sponsors in managing employer-sponsored retirement plans.
- An insurance agent conducts business and transacts (recommends) investment products within the limit of packaged investment products, such as mutual funds or annuities.
- A robo-adviser is an automated online system that offers an algorithm-based portfolio management service at a low cost and with minimal human interaction; it is registered as a RIA and can be a hybrid model with the option to add human adviser assistance.

B/D firms can be categorized as National, Regional, Independent, or Bank. Wirehouse B/D advisers and Independent B/D advisers have different operational systems and thus different services they can (or prefer to) recommend to clients. Technically speaking, an Investment Adviser Representative (IAR) is a person while a Registered Investment Adviser (RIA) is a firm, but they are used interchangeably. A hybrid RIA is often confused with a dually registered adviser, but the former operates separately for RIA and B/D business while the latter operates under the same B/D as well as B/D's corporate

RIA channel. Let's say you wanted to open two different types of accounts (i.e., fee-based account vs. commission-based account); having each account in different entities is how hybrid RIAs operate, whereas keeping two different types of accounts separately under one entity is similar to how dually registered advisers operate. RIAs and B/Ds have different registration requirements with regulatory organizations, which also vary by the state or the managed asset size. Some are exempt from registration requirements under a specific circumstance.

A person who doesn't manage money but refers clients to another firm as a solicitor can also call himself or herself a financial adviser as long as the license requirement is met and the agreement is disclosed to clients. As you can see, it's simply impossible to know what any of these people can truly offer you, as an investor, without comprehensive research.

Unfortunately, many investors lump all financial professionals into one broad group. When Bernie Madoff's Ponzi scheme news was released back in 2009, I encountered many investors who were worried about the safety of their money—even though the majority of their holdings were in mutual funds. A Ponzi scheme is a fraudulent business practice that pays investors with other investors' money. Therefore, it's a circulation of money from one investor to another, not a return of investment. This fraud was based on an unregistered hedge fund operation. On the other hand, mutual funds are registered with the Securities and Exchange Commission (SEC) and regulated under the Investment Company Act of 1940. Hedge funds and mutual funds are totally different entities. The concerns related to extensive fraud could have been the general perception of low investor confidence in the financial industry itself, but the reality is that investors don't know enough about the basic differences among diverse financial professionals.

As a result of events like this, investors have unrealistic expectations and deep concerns, which have a negative impact on long-term sustainability in investing. A financial planner is neither a hedge fund manager nor a stock guru. And a day trader is neither a wealth manager nor a retirement plan adviser. When you decide to work with a financial professional, one of the initial steps is to understand his or her expertise and capability as well as how the firm operates.

The Financial Industry Regulatory Authority (FINRA), mentioned in the previous chapters, has a resource known as **BrokerCheck**. Investors can start here when seeking information about potential financial professionals. You can see the employment history, licenses, and if there are any relevant disclosure events or outside business activities. The Securities and Exchange Commission (SEC) website has another excellent information-gathering resource known as the **EDGAR Search Tool** (for more detail, see **Appendix D—Resources**). Whenever you encounter unfamiliar information, you are well-advised to use a search engine to learn more or seek advice from someone who can answer your questions. It's a necessary step to prevent the common mistake of not knowing whom you work with.

Don't Assume Your Financial Professional Knows Everything

Let's say you work with an insurance or tax agent. Now, imagine that you need to roll over your retirement account but have never worked with a financial professional. Be sure to do your homework before you turn in your retirement account to that agent. While the agent may also call himself or herself a financial adviser, he or she may not be the best choice for your long-term outlook. If you're looking for advice on retirement planning, you may be able to find a financial professional with superior expertise in that area—and it's possible that your agent has expertise in wealth management. Either way, what matters is that you do your research before handing over your money to anyone.

Let's use this example a bit more. Consider that you initially were looking for retirement planning guidance, but you've started hearing about high returns in *private equity* funds or *managed futures*. Does your financial professional claim to possess expertise in this area? Did you expect your adviser to be an expert in that area as well simply because he or she is in the investment industry? Are you certain that you didn't create an impossible or hard-to-achieve expectation?

Overgeneralization and a disregard of differences among financial professionals cause investors to make poor choices when choosing to work with someone. Naturally, they build unrealistic expectations into their investment outcomes, and that will ultimately lead to dissatisfaction and reduced confidence. In a situation like this, though, the negative result comes from picking the wrong financial professional, which is also considered a poor investment decision.

Just as in a pre-employment screening procedure where applicants undergo background checks, including education and past work experience, investors need to pre-screen potential financial professionals. Before having a face-to-face meeting, you should get to know the adviser you're considering by looking at his or her credentials and qualifications. It's dangerous to just take someone's word or to hire someone because you like him or her. Remember, a claim is different from a fact, and kindness and ethics are two very different things.

Parting Thoughts

The investment universe is vast, and so is the world of financial professionals. We've covered the importance of knowing your goal and risk tolerance as well as methods for selecting investments that are suitable for you, given the enormity of the investment universe. This logic is also extended to working with financial professionals, given the diversity of the financial professional universe. You must fully engage in the due diligence process for both investment products and financial professionals. It's imperative that you acknowledge others' expertise appropriately and build reasonable expectations accordingly.

Selection and Expectation: Keep in mind that financial professionals possess diverse expertise and operate their businesses under different systems. It's critical to know who you work with; choose the right financial professional and set up reasonable expectations.

CHAPTER FOURTEEN

INVESTMENT OPTIONS— WHAT ARE THE ODDS OF ONE COMPANY MAKING THE BEST PRODUCT FOR EVERYTHING?

We use various products in our everyday routine. More than likely, your office supplies and bath products come from different companies. Each company and product has its niche market. Your selection criteria also differ based on the object. You may choose to save money on toilet paper and spend more on high-quality food items. What are the chances of your favorite cereal brand also making the best pillowcase? Because there are numerous investments available, what are the odds of one company producing the best investment for everything? Review your investment holdings to find out if they are limited to just a few companies. If they are, the reasons for such choices should be valid and justifiable.

Beware of Limiting Your Options Voluntarily

If you're inside a mall or an airport, there are a limited number of places to dine. You may be able to find something you like without any issue, but you won't have many choices. Similarly, if you own an insurance product or participate in an employer-sponsored retirement plan, you may have limited investment options. In these cases, you must look for the best opportunities you can find among available options. Other-wise, it doesn't make sense to limit your investment choices voluntarily without a compelling reason to do so.

For instance, let's say you want to take advantage of a *breakpoint discount* of a *load mutual fund*. A mutual fund has multiple share classes with different fee structures and features, which are designed to attract a wide variety of investors. When you buy a *front-end load mutual fund*, the total invested amount must be above the set limit in order to receive a breakpoint discount for the load under the same family. For that specific purpose, you may choose to construct your entire portfolio with one family of funds. But what if another fund from a different fund family fits your portfolio more effectively, or a combination of *no-load mutual funds* from different fund families results in a better-built portfolio? You'd also choose to invest in various Exchange-Trade Funds (ETFs) with lower expenses than mutual funds. For more detail, see **Appendix C—Glossary**.

Many other alternatives exist, and the best choice is ultimately up to each investor. Nevertheless, the benefits should be compelling enough to justify the reasons for voluntarily limiting your options or ignoring a wide range of available choices. Don't limit your investment choices unless the derived benefits are greater than the drawbacks or restrictions; it will ultimately limit your success in investing.

Beware of Having Your Options Limited Intentionally

Investors pay professionals for their services, and diverse money managers, agents, and advisers work in companies with different structures and platforms. Wholesalers from various investment companies also promote their products to the public; the list of widely used products includes, but is not limited to:

- Stocks and bonds
- Open- or closed-end mutual funds
- Exchange-Traded Products (ETPs)
- Insurance products, such as annuities and life insurance
- Unlisted Business Development Companies (BDCs)
- Non-traded Real Estate Investment Trusts (REITs)
- Private placements or equities or funds

- Managed futures
- Structured products
- Unit Investment Trusts (UITs)

Generally, wholesalers work with financial professionals so that they can reach out to consumers in the end. After all, individual investors are the target market for investment products.

For instance, each Broker/Dealer (B/D) firm has different "approved" product lists. Investment companies may compensate the B/D firm to be included in its product lists; this type of payment is called "shelf space" payment as it's like putting the product on the shelf at the store. Imagine going to a grocery store. In order for you to be able to buy a certain product, the grocery store has to offer it first by putting it on the shelf. If the store doesn't carry enough inventory or offers lower-quality products, you can go to other stores to find better deals. The investment industry works in a similar way. "Trailing" commissions or "revenue-sharing" arrangements are very common, but it's up to you to stay (if it's reasonable) or look for better options (if it's unfair) as an investor.

Let's assume a financial adviser has a working relationship with ABC mutual fund company. The wholesaler visits the adviser on a regular basis to share updates and promotions for their products. If the adviser sells more of that company's mutual funds, the wholesaler's compensation is increased accordingly. Therefore, the wholesaler is motivated to "help" the adviser in any manner so that ABC mutual funds can be sold more frequently to the adviser's clients. The adviser uses client appreciation dinners or seminars to interact with clients and provide customer service. Those events are often paid for by ABC wholesaler under the umbrella of marketing support.

It works like a business partnership. The compensation of the whole-saler grows if the adviser sells more ABC mutual funds. The adviser also has a chance to provide pleasant dinners or seminars with clients at no cost while maintaining a higher level of customer service. These events also help a business retain its positive image. Even if it's just a simple update meeting without monetary support, an adviser may favor ABC mutual funds over others for the sake of the business rela-tionship. Or the brokerage firm may offer *proprietary funds* and give incentives to the adviser who sells its own proprietary funds. Therefore, the adviser may have extra incentives for using those funds. For more detail, see **Appendix C—Glossary**.

However, it becomes problematic, even unethical, if ABC mutual funds or the proprietary funds are not the best product for clients or are used excessively to favor a business partner (or to take advantage of marketing support or incentives). This is how your portfolio can end up with only a limited number of products from a handful of companies—even though you never put any restrictions in place voluntarily.

For the sake of an example, let's say the adviser put the majority of your money into ABC mutual funds or the proprietary funds even though they weren't the best fit for your portfolio. You might not notice that anything is wrong and may be content with regular dinners and thank-you cards. But what if you noticed that most of your hold-ings were from ABC mutual fund company or the firm's proprietary funds and inquired about the reason behind such construction? If you discovered that the holdings were not in your best interest, you would probably choose to work with another adviser.

A business is a business, but there is a fine line between being business-savvy and unethical. A financial *service* industry is also an industry that provides customer *service*. Understanding how the business works will help you hone your awareness and recognize when something isn't right.

Parting Thoughts

In order to make a choice amid various options, you should be aware of all the benefits and drawbacks of different products as well as how products are delivered to you. If your investment options are limited, and it's not in your best interest, it's time to make changes. Every investor is capable of making changes and should do so whenever necessary, so pay close attention to what you own. Awareness makes all the difference.

Investment Options: Understand if your investment holdings are limited to a small number of companies. If they are, derived benefits should be compelling enough to support such a choice.

CHAPTER FIFTEEN

DUE DILIGENCE— HOW DID YOU GET A REFERRAL?

Have you ever rented an apartment from a company that offered you an incentive for a referral, such as a discount on your next month's rent? If so, you might have recommended your complex to a friend because you like where you live and/or wanted to receive that discount. In the end, it's your friend's responsibility to do the homework on where to live and decide which apartment is the best fit. Likewise, as an investor, you need to thoroughly perform your due diligence when considering referrals for a financial professional.

Learn Why You're Receiving a Referral

If one adviser refers you to another, chances are good that the original adviser has something to gain monetarily by making the referral. To understand how this works, you need to learn about the *book*. Financial advisers build close relationships with clients, and the relationship has value, not just for investors but for other financial professionals or operating firms. In some cases, advisers take their *book* with them when they move to a different firm. The *book* includes their client list and the amount of assets under their management. Sometimes advisers even get paid to go to other firms due to the high value of their *book*.

When a financial adviser decides to exit the business entirely, he or she might sell the *book* to another adviser. What does this mean? It means all the clients he or she used to work with are referred to the new adviser who bought the *book*. There is usually a payment arrangement between the two parties, but the client retention rate after the transition can affect the *book's* value in the form of monetary compensation to the former adviser. Therefore, the seller of the *book* has an incentive to recommend the new adviser (buyer of the *book*) to former clients. An adviser can also work as a solicitor for the firm, thereby referring clients and sharing the compensation with the firm.

Additionally, many professionals build business relationships by working as a team because teamwork brings about a great deal of efficiency. Financial advisers may refer clients to other professionals (who are typically involved in wealth management), such as tax or legal practices. In return, estate-planning lawyers or tax specialists may refer their clients to the advisers who gave them referrals.

Selling the *book,* being a solicitor, or working as a team are simply ways of doing business (as long as it's within ethical standards). However, it is up to investors to recognize possible conflicts of interest and identify the real reason behind the referral. You can start with a direct question such as, "Will you receive any compensation for this referral?" FINRA's **BrokerCheck** (discussed in **Chapter Thirteen**) is also a must for doing a basic background check. Don't just take the referral at face value; it's up to you to find out what is best for you as an investor.

True Talent or Marketing Skill?

Some celebrities land major movie roles or release music albums simply because they're famous, not necessarily because they're talented. They are broadly recognized (and thus marketable to the public) because of their fame and publicity. Unfortunately, many gifted artists don't have a chance to shine because they've never been given an opportunity to prove their talents—or they are just not good at marketing themselves. It's important to remember that a positive reputation may come from being talented, but it can also be the result of marketing disguised as skill.

Think of it this way: anyone can appear on a television or radio show as a spokesperson if he or she is willing to pay for it. It's like product placement in the movie industry. A projected image is delivered in a subtle way (referred to as "sponsored content"), but the audience may assume that he or she must be an expert if the person is "famous" enough to be on TV or radio. As an investor, you need to be attentive to these possibilities to avoid being misled.

Answering the following questions will help you discern the motivation behind the referral or reputation:

- How did you choose your financial professional?
- Was it through a referral from a person who you know, and does he or she receive some type of compensation for this referral?
- Is it because an advertisement or appearance seemed impressive?
- Did the publicity give you a sense of assurance that he or she was the right person to advise you?

When it comes to investing, you have too much to lose if you base your decisions on false judgments or presumptions.

Dealing with People's Wealth

Before you choose to work with financial professionals, you need to fully comprehend their skills and abilities; the consequences, after all, can affect your future negatively. When you understand a financial professional's true capability, you can choose the right expert to work with and set up reasonable and realistic expectations, which will eventually help you to remain a long-term investor.

The Chartered Financial Analyst (CFA) Institute leads the **Future of Finance** project, including an education initiative called **Putting Investors First** (from a financial professional's standpoint) and created a document known as a **Statement of Investor Rights** (from an investor's standpoint), with the purpose of "providing tools to empower the world of finance to commit to fairness, improved understanding, and personal integrity."

You can also find valuable information about what to look for as an investor by visiting the Securities and Exchange Commission (SEC) website if you are unsure of where to start. Check out the **Investor Publications** tab and review the document entitled **Protect Your Money: Check out Brokers and Investment Advisers**. For more detail, see **Appendix D—Resources**.

Investing involves dealing with people's wealth, and its impact can change people's lives. And both professionals and investors have the right and carry the burden of responsibility.

Parting Thoughts

Investing involves researching not only the right investment tools and products, but also the right financial professionals with whom you choose to work. It's your right and duty to conduct research and determine a financial professional's competency and ethical standards.

Due Diligence: Do not rely solely on referrals or reputation when choosing a financial professional. It is your responsibility to conduct thorough research, utilizing detailed selection criteria before you hand over your money to someone else.

CHAPTER SIXTEEN

COMMUNICATION— WHAT KIND OF SHOES WOULD YOU LIKE TO BUY?

When you buy shoes at a store, you tell the sales representative your size as well as what you're looking for. You pick the color you want, and you specify if your perfect pair is meant for daily wear or a special occasion. You also share details regarding comfort and appearance. Communicating in detail helps you get what you want. Why wouldn't you do the same thing for your investments? It's important to keep the communication flowing with your financial professional.

Speak Before You Buy

All too often, investors fail to get involved enough in the investing process. They may leave key decisions to their financial professionals and go along with recommendations without sufficiently understanding what they are about to own. Frequently, retail investors are surprised by an illiquid investment, which is not eligible to sell upon their request due to the imposed restriction on liquidation. Hence, when the investors want to sell the holding, it might not be redeemable (or might have to be sold with a penalty or at a deep discount). Some people are misled by salespeople; some don't fully understand the imposed restriction, and others are simply unaware of what kind of investment it was at the time of purchase. The bottom line is that they didn't know enough about the investment (or financial professional) *before* making the purchase.

Let's revisit the earlier analogy. You save and put aside money to buy a new pair of shoes for yourself, and then you communicate your needs effectively to the sales representative who has the knowledge in terms of material, inventory, etc. It's more important to know what shoes are right for you *before* you've bought them, not after the purchase. The same goes for your investments. Ask all the questions you need and find out the details about your investments *before* making a decision. Proactive involvement is important to make sure the suggested recommendations are right for you. Looking at investment mistakes in hindsight is something you want to avoid.

Monitor After You Hire

Most investors are guarded and wary of trusting anyone initially; but once they've built a relationship with a financial professional, they tend to lose that caution and fail to pay attention to the ongoing process. The reasons vary; it could be because they don't know what to ask, or perhaps they feel embarrassed by asking too many basic questions. And some people simply have faith and don't want to push their financial professionals. If you've invested poorly in the past, it's possible that you felt the process was too complicated, so you opted not to get too involved. And in some cases, investors honestly believe it's not their job to conduct research or ask questions. After all, that's the reason why they hired someone else to manage their money.

While regular client appreciation dinners and update meetings are nice, those events are hardly proof that your investments are being well taken care of (and in your best interest). As an investor, you need to remain in charge of your money. Do not hesitate to speak your mind and present your point of view when you work with a financial professional. Monitoring your investments (or your financial professional) is a nonstop process.

Communication Is a Two-Way Street

Investment discussions should consist of two-way communication, not a one-sided monologue delivered by a financial professional, telling you what to do and what's best for you. Ask for clarification directly with a straightforward approach. Here are some questions to get you started:

- Are there any possible conflicts of interest?
- What type of compensation do you receive if I accept this recommendation? Is it an up-front commission, or is it built into a fee-based account?
- What costs are associated with this investment? Can you give me a full breakdown?
- What is the expected holding period, and is there any lockup period?
- What is the liquidation process, and does it carry an early redemption fee?
- Is it a suitable investment for me right now?
- What documents require my signature? Are they explained in detail?

This list of questions could go on and on, and you should also make your financial professional aware of any *material* changes you'll be making, such as a near-term lump-sum withdrawal/deposit or retirement plan change or even health issues that would affect your financial status. Your questions can be simply, "What is it?" or "How does it work?" You may just be asking yourself these questions to find out what needs to be explained in the investing process for the sake of curiosity. The more you know, the more you are in charge.

Once you express what you are looking for, you can rely on the financial professional's expertise and knowledge—but it's critical to make a concerted effort to communicate and understand your investments. Let financial professionals take the lead, but voice your needs and make it clear that you have a say in every single decision that concerns your money. If there are no concerns, you can still offer upfront feedback. Essential details, such as the alignment of interest or built-in embedded costs, are more likely to be skipped and hidden, unless you take charge and let your interests be known. Do not let someone else decide what's right for you without adequate communication.

Initiate the discussion with your financial professional. Don't shy away from asking any questions; all of them have value (and none of them are pointless). A few seemingly trivial questions could hold significant answers when making an investment decision.

Parting Thoughts

You don't have to possess expertise and in-depth knowledge in investing, but you do need to have a proper understanding of your investments (or financial professional). You can trust who you work with, but always stay closely involved in how your money's managed. Reserve your right as an investor; it is your money, after all! The consequences of investment choices are too critical to discount.

Communication: Keep the communication line open while working with a financial professional. It's important to know what you are about to invest in *before* you buy rather than be surprised by it *after* the purchase.

CHAPTER SEVENTEEN

REVIEW AND ASSESSMENT— WHEN WAS THE LAST TIME YOU GOT NEW QUOTES FOR YOUR INSURANCE?

No one likes the process of shopping around and getting quotes for services or products. It's time-consuming and tedious to contact companies when you're looking for a good deal on insurance or trying to find a more reputable company. In the long run, though, you are better off with a product that suits you best. Even if you stay with your current provider, it is still a good idea to research and confirm current rates. The same goes for your investments as well as the work of your financial professional. Examine your investments and how they're managed on a regular basis and explore second opinions (if necessary). It's essential to stay cognizant of your investing process as an ongoing duty.

Intuitive Read vs. Thorough Inspection

Many people search for new insurance only when their current insurance premium goes up—and some don't even bother to do that. The same thing happens when portfolio performance is acceptable (or better). Investors don't care about their investments nearly as much as when the value goes down—especially below a certain threshold. When portfolio values go up, many investors are satisfied with the progress and are eager to find out how much money they've made so far. Without any further assessment, they feel confident that their financial professional has done an excellent job.

On the other hand, if portfolio values decrease substantially, investors don't want to know how much money they've lost since it's hard to deal with the truth (referred to as "unopened envelope syndrome"). Without any further assessment, investors may feel doubtful about the quality of a financial professional's work. However, this assessment relies on intuition instead of reasonable evidence. A loss in your portfolio's value may not be indicative of poor advice from your financial professional. Depending solely on investment performance, especially short-term, is not a proper way of evaluating the quality of work regarding your investments. This is based on emotions, and investment decisions, including the review process, shouldn't be emotional (as mentioned throughout the book).

You shouldn't assume your current insurance serves your needs just because you've had it for a long time (or because the premium has remained the same). Don't assume your investments are in your best interest without a thorough inspection. Whether there is friction or not, it's necessary to examine your investments in a timely manner and stay involved in the ongoing process.

Assessment Is a Must, Not an Option

Review and assessment are required for reality checks, which enhance your awareness and knowledge as a whole. It's just as important to confirm that your investment approach is appropriate and also that your financial professional is working in your best interest. By checking this periodically, you can find better alternatives, if necessary.

If you realize your ability to invest alone didn't work out as intended, you're well advised to broaden your choices and consider working with a qualified financial professional. If you continue to ignore this need, bigger issues will catch up with you eventually. Don't wait until you learn your lesson the hard way. Would you rather wait until the truth reveals itself and deal with negative consequences or take charge in the process and face facts now?

Once you decide that change is inevitable, you may feel disappointed and uncertain about how to proceed. And yet, the hassle and irritation are only minor inconveniences in the big picture. Use any tension you feel as motivation to put your time and effort to good use in a constructive way. And consider getting a second opinion. They're often helpful when taking a comprehensive look at your investments. Second opinions reveal new information and provide different perspectives. Feedback from an outside party is always an opportunity for you to address things in terms of how your money is managed.

When seeking a third-party's assessment for the second opinion, typically you are asked to bring the statements of your account. That's because these periodic statements contain fairly detailed information, which is generally more than just the beginning and ending account value that most investors focus on. It lists all the holdings with gains and losses, usually broken down by *asset classes*. It also contains a transaction history, dividend reinvestment setup (either dividends are reinvested into the holding or put into cash), and fee deductions. Learn to scrutinize your statements instead of just checking the change in total value. A third party can provide you with a new perspective on your investments, but the review process is what you need to do on a constant basis nonetheless.

If you work with a financial professional, you should be having update meetings on a regular basis. Take notes during (or right after) the meeting while your memory is fresh. It's like taking notes when you were in school: it helps when you are studying for an exam (or contemplating a change in approach). Revisit the discussion and monitor things closely to ensure that any necessary steps have been completed within the promised time frame. Check if there is any confusion or discrepancy between recommendations and your holdings. Double check the responses you received. Did you get the detailed answers you hoped for—or did you simply receive vague or general updates?

Make sure the implementation was aligned with previously discussed points from the meeting. These are valuable clues and help you assess your financial professional's work without any outside assistance.

You can give credit where it's deserved or decide to make necessary changes if you discover anything that does not feel like it is in your best interest. Complaints and emotional confrontations are hurtful and fruitless, but silence and inaction are more harmful in the end—especially if nothing changes when changes are needed. A candid and constructive discussion can help you discover what needs to be modified. As an investor, you have many other options and solutions to improve your current status.

Importance of Review and Rebalance

Investing is a continuous cycle: portfolio construction, implementation, review, rebalance, implementation, and review again. You may skip one or two steps due to lack of necessity, but you should have at least one step involved as long as you stay in investing. In other words, you still need to review your portfolio on a regular basis even when you do not plan to make changes. Therefore, even the most passive style of investing needs a review process at minimum.

The process of review and rebalance is a step of preparing for the future while learning from the past. An investor reviews a portfolio in order to reflect back on the choices that have already been made (past) as well as to evaluate what kind of new decisions are necessary to move forward (future). It is critical to check and ensure the viability of on-going progress to reach your ultimate goal in investing, but the method doesn't have to be prescheduled or preset. The frequency and timing of the review and rebalance process should be customized to fit the scope of your personal priorities.

Parting Thoughts

It's always advantageous to check what you have and what else is available. Whether you manage your own money or work with a financial professional, it's essential to review and evaluate your investments (or your financial professional's work) on a regular basis.

Review and Assessment: Examine your investments regularly, take necessary steps to follow up on your assessment, and look for second opinions (if necessary). You can take control of how your money is managed when you remain involved throughout the process.

CHAPTER EIGHTEEN

CLOSING THOUGHTS— THE SMART INVESTOR

Investing requires intensive work and commitment. Knowledge boosts confidence and credibility, but the hardest part of all is putting your knowledge into practice. It's like a New Year's resolution. You need to do more than just say you're going to do something. You must plan and then act on that plan.

The best advice is the simplest: take one step at a time. The true benefits of investing are entirely up to you. Acknowledge your investing level and work to improve your knowledge, so you can invest properly. Take stock of your priorities and take the time to consider all your options with prudence. Your chosen investment method should be based on your personal goals and should provide the proper solution to ensure you achieve them.

Remember, investing is not about becoming richer. Investing is done to accumulate wealth in a sustainable way for increased prosperity throughout different stages of your life. Investing is a way of taking control of your financial security, but don't get seduced by the allure of "easy money." Shortcuts may make things easier, but long-term sustainability does not come from such practices.

A smart investor is not a perfectionist; instead, he or she is willing to learn from the past and move forward with a new perspective. A smart investor doesn't sprint. He or she sees the long-term goal and undertakes an approach like a marathon runner. Skillful marathon runners know how to pace themselves with reasonable time management and persistent practice. Smart investors are disciplined planners and determined pursuers. In the end, they gain intelligence by proactively trying to become better at investing.

Importance of Overcoming Emotions

Behavioral finance emphasizes our emotions' significant impact on investment outcomes as well as investors' behaviors. It also explains the drawbacks of being emotionally involved with investment decisions as many investors suffer from shortsighted emotional reactions. The common result is selling an investment at a low price (fear-driven) or buying it at a high price (greed-driven). Emotionally-driven decisions also result in investments going oversold or overbought, which creates additional volatility. You've probably heard the phrase, "Greed and fear drive the investment market." Fear (risk-focused) and greed (return-focused) drive investors to make irrational decisions. We know that we need to keep those emotions out of the decision-making process, but that's incredibly difficult to do.

Fear of losing your money keeps you from investing and undermines your confidence. And if you've suffered repeated losses, you may have unconsciously shifted your priorities to protect your current wealth instead of thinking of the long-term goal or benefits of investing. You may have also developed a *status quo bias*, choosing to keep everything just the way it is (i.e., not investing) instead of taking chances.

In the field of *neuroeconomics*, researchers study the role emotions play in the financial decision-making process (as well as the consequences of that behavior). It shows how natural it is for our brain to affect financial decisions. Accepting emotions is a difficult task as we may feel that it's a sign of weakness, but keep in mind that it's natural to feel emotions. The focus should be on how to overcome them.

The key is to accept the issue and figure out how to keep your emotions from interfering with an investment decision. What matters the most to you as an investor is not the same for everyone, and it can't be determined by anyone but you. You need to concentrate on yourself as an investor more than on what's happening around you to overcome these emotions. Acknowledge what matters the most to you and build a long-term plan to invest with discipline.

Prioritize to Strategize

We can bring about change, but it's difficult to alter who we are at our core, that is, our fundamental qualities. Everyone has different priorities and goals to achieve and emotions to control. One solution doesn't work for everyone.

It's critical to acknowledge what you *can* and *cannot* take (or do) in investing. If you ignore your priorities, it's difficult to cope with different levels of uncertainty and surprise in investing, which leads to making emotional decisions. "I want to make more money (greed) but do not want to lose (fear)" is not a constructive statement. You need to prioritize your goals and needs in order to strategize an appropriate action plan.

Recognizing your priorities creates discipline and efficiency. It also helps you to achieve positive momentum and maintain emotional balance throughout the investing process. Figure out what you value the most, what you need to overcome, and how you are going to achieve your goal. Make the investing method fit you, not the other way around. Prioritize what you need the most and strategize how to achieve your goals on a regular basis. These are the not so secret practices that lead to smart investing.

APPENDIX A—SUMMARY

Recognize your current status in investing and develop essential knowledge to understand the process and steps so that you can identify the next thing you must do to move forward. The following is a summary of the 17 points covered in this book. Each key concept was illustrated in a text bubble at the end of each chapter.

1. **Goal Setting**: Establish your investing goal in detail and select a practical action plan accordingly. Proper goal setting is a prerequisite to building a functioning plan.

2. **Risk Tolerance**: Acknowledge your suitable risk tolerance level in terms of both ability and willingness to take a risk respectively. You don't have to take risks you're not comfortable with just because you can (ability). Correspondingly, you shouldn't take a risk that is beyond your ability simply because you want to (willingness).

3. **Investing Capability**: Accept your investing capability honestly and do not confuse the impact of uncontrollable factors with your ability. Feeling confident about your investing capability is different from overestimating or misunderstanding what you can do.

4. **Investment Evaluation**: Analyze each individual investment by taking your existing holdings into consideration from the total portfolio's perspective. Your current portfolio and personal situation define what's right for you regardless of the attractiveness of an investment.

5. **Investments with Emotional Ties**: Do not confuse familiarity with the true value of an investment. When a positive bias due to familiarity turns into an unconditional rationalization, any information will be immediately filtered via a biased view (jeopardizing objectivity). It's also important to

understand the difference between an emotionally attached investment (need to avoid) and the soft value of an investment (need to accept).

6. **Portfolio Construction**: Broaden your investment options by researching what exists between the *extremes* of growth and income (or safety). A variety of investments with different characteristics exist, and the utilization of all the different levels brings about higher efficiency in investing.

7. **Portfolio Review**: Focus on the big picture goals of your overall portfolio during the review process, so you avoid making emotional decisions. Investment decisions shouldn't be based on spontaneous reactions and trivial details.

8. **Strategy and Implementation**: Do not let your passionate conviction interfere with your objectivity. Strong beliefs are valuable as long as they don't lead to excessive usage and a mind adverse to alternatives. You can maximize the benefits of your choices with balanced judgment and usage.

9. **Research**: Distinguish a fact from an opinion during the research process. A smart researcher is receptive to various recommendations but knows how to assess the grounds of an opinion and the reliability of a fact.

10. **Valuation**: Do not choose an investment simply because it's discounted. The fair value must be determined in order to measure the accurate discount value, given its cost structure. Investment decisions shouldn't be made based on incomplete information that is presented to you as a good deal.

11. **Investment Decision**: Do not make an assumption about the content of the investment just based on its name. If you do, you can easily misidentify the strategy and unintentionally end up with an investment that is unsuitable for you.

12. **Diversification**: Explore and take advantage of all the investment opportunities within the scope of your capability (or your financial professional's capability). Proper diversification helps produce positive outcomes while reducing the total risk in a portfolio.

13. **Selection and Expectation**: Keep in mind that financial professionals possess diverse expertise and operate their businesses under different systems. It's critical to know who you work with; choose the right financial professional and set up reasonable expectations.

14. **Investment Options**: Understand if your investment holdings are limited to a small number of companies. If they are, derived benefits should be compelling enough to support such a choice.

15. **Due Diligence**: Do not rely solely on referrals or reputation when choosing a financial professional. It is your responsibility to conduct thorough research, utilizing detailed selection criteria before you hand over your money to someone else.

16. **Communication**: Keep the communication line open while working with a financial professional. It's important to know what you are about to invest in *before* you buy rather than be surprised by it *after* the purchase.

17. **Review and Assessment**: Examine your investments regularly, take necessary steps to follow up on your assessment, and look for second opinions (if necessary). You can take control of how your money is managed when you remain involved throughout the process.

APPENDIX B——REVIEW

We are more receptive to learning when we know we can benefit from that newfound knowledge. The more you understand how investing works, the better you can invest. The following is a summary of the essential knowledge discussed in this book in the form of formulas, comparisons, and Q&As.

Review as Formulas

a. Return = (Price change + Income) – Cost

An income-producing investment enhances a return while associated costs erode a return. The true return to an investor is the net of all the fees and costs, including the tax and opportunity cost. Hence, a low-cost (or tax-efficient) investment with income increases the final bottom-line return.

- Pay attention to income stream rather than just price change.
- Acknowledge (and evaluate) fees paid for the products and services and build a cost-efficient portfolio considering tax consequences.

b. Higher Return per a Risk (Unit of Return/Unit of Risk) Lower Risk per a Return (Unit of Risk/Unit of Return)

An investment is considered to be attractive when it has a higher expected return per a risk or a lower risk per a return (based on Optimal Portfolio of the Efficient Frontier). An investor wouldn't take additional risks if they didn't lead to extra returns. He or she would, likewise, never accept a lower return that doesn't lead to a safer outcome. In other words, expected returns should be higher than an embedded risk, and the risk you are taking should be justifiable based on the expected return.

- Measure the return potential for a unit of risk to maximize your return.
- Explore the best possible low-risk options for a unit of return to minimize your risk.

c. Intrinsic Value – Discount = Undervalued
Intrinsic Value + Premium = Overvalued

An undervalued investment presents a buying opportunity since you are paying a lower price than its fair value; thereby, you have a greater chance to capture higher upside potential. In a valuation process, identifying an investment's fair value is a prerequisite to determining if an investment is undervalued or overvalued. And the reason for the price change is more important than the level of the change itself.

- Identify the intrinsic value of an investment in order to decide what to buy (undervalued) and sell (overvalued).
- Research "why" in comparison with "how much" in terms of price change.

d. True Value = Absolute Value + Relative Value

Absolute value is calculated on a stand-alone basis, and it's either improved or deteriorated by its relative value. The benefits of a product may have more worth to you than to others when your personal need increases its relative value (meaning it's more valuable to you regardless of its absolute value). An investment product works the same way. The true value of an investment is determined by not only its attractiveness (absolute), but also how it interacts with other variables—including an investor's existing portfolio and personal situation (relative).

- Analyze the value of an investment as a part of your portfolio given your priorities in order to incorporate both absolute and relative value.
- Diversify your portfolio to capitalize on its relative value, such as diversification benefits.

Review as Comparisons

a. Passive vs. Active Money Management

- Simplicity vs. Complexity (in terms of structure)
- Cost-sensitive vs. Risk-sensitive (in terms of investor profile)
- Cost-efficient vs. Expertise-efficient (in terms of advantage)

b. Strategic vs. Tactical Asset Allocation

- Long-term vs. Short-term (in terms of time horizon)
- Core vs. Satellite (in terms of portfolio construction)
- Target vs. Opportunity (in terms of main strategy)

c. Fundamental vs. Technical Analysis

- Intrinsic value vs. Past price movement (in terms of emphasis)
- Forward-looking vs. Backward-looking (in terms of valuation perspective)
- Valuation vs. Probability (in terms of analysis focus)

d. Systematic vs. Unsystematic Risk

- Non-diversifiable vs. Diversifiable (in terms of risk management)
- Overall market vs. Specific (in terms of scope)
- Compensable vs. Non-compensable (in terms of portfolio return perspective)

e. Growth vs. Value Investing

- Justifiable premium vs. Mispriced discount (in terms of valuation style)
- Higher perceived risk vs. Lower perceived risk (in terms of risk perception)
- In-favor vs. Out-of-favor (in terms of price level)

Review as Q&A

Question: How do I know my risk tolerance level?

Answer: You know your risk tolerance level better than anyone else, and yet it's hard to recognize and/or describe it. As discussed previously, your risk tolerance level is broken down into two components: your ability to take a risk and your willingness to take a risk. The ability to take a risk is relatively easy to measure because it's based on wealth; however, the willingness to take a risk is often distorted by the fear of losing money or the temptation to chase after a higher return. Willingness to take a risk is a fundamental quality of your own nature as an investor rather than something you'd change based on other factors.

One of the easiest ways to learn about your willingness to take a risk is to acknowledge your reaction to negative returns (to measure loss aversion). A portfolio's objective reflects an investor's risk tolerance level, so be aware of which objective you select. An *Aggressive Growth* objective means you have a high-risk tolerance level, while a *Preservation of Capital* objective means you have a low-risk tolerance level. Realistically speaking, you shouldn't have a *Growth* objective if you can't take a negative 10% return because holdings in a *Growth* objective are more likely to move up and down closely with the market, meaning a higher volatility. Review it on a regular basis to discover your risk tolerance level; it evolves with your *life cycle* and any relevant *material* events in your life.

Question: Why do I need a portfolio?

Answer: We use a variety of necessities to enrich our lifestyle. Imagine trying to live with only one or two of them! It would be extremely difficult and challenging to maintain a decent quality of life with just shelter and food but no water. Having excess necessities is also unnecessary and costly (without added benefits). Portfolio construction works in a similar way. As an investor, you need a portfolio that consists of suitable investments that are designed to reach your goal. You need a portfolio with different "necessities" to implement your functioning investment plan.

A portfolio doesn't have to include a specific number of different *asset classes* as long as it provides much-needed diversification at your level. At the same time, you do need "necessities" to build a working portfolio. More importantly, portfolio construction is required for effective risk management. An investor can manage the total risk effectively and practically in the context of a portfolio, but not in an individual holding. Risk management is not about reducing fluctuation or volatility; it's about how prepared you are (and can be) under different scenarios that could affect your financial security.

Question: How do I know what's the best way to invest?

Answer: Think of an investing method like a meal plan. Based on your personal situation, the right plan for you will differ from that of someone else. Your meal plan also changes based on your condition over time—and so does the best investment method. If you have high cholesterol, your meal plan should target lowering your cholesterol level. If you've been eating the same type of food for too long, it's important to mix it up with options that offer a wide range of nutrition. And if you can't build a meal plan on your own, you should seek a professional's guidance. On a similar note, if you are risk averse, a concentrated investment with high risk is unsuitable—regardless of the expected return potential. If you don't have the capability to invest on your own, it's worthwhile to work with a financial professional rather than participate in self-directed investing.

In conclusion, overgeneralization is dangerous. Mimicking another's method or trying to find the best investing method is a waste of time unless you know yourself as an investor in the first place. Prioritize to strategize; everyone has different priorities and the best investment method lies inside the parameter of your priorities.

Question: Why do I need to stay in investing long-term?

Answer: Investing is like building a healthy lifestyle. It's continuous and requires effort and patience. Being on a diet temporarily won't change your long-term health if your life-style is still filled with unhealthy habits. And your health will be fine even though you indulge in so-called guilty plea-sures once in a while, as long as you try to maintain a healthy lifestyle overall. Think of short-term performance as eating a salad or a cookie, and long-term performance as overall well-being. Of course, the extent and duration matters, too, but short-term performance or one bad experience shouldn't prevent you from staying in investing in the long run. Investing continues to evolve with your life; it is designed to be long-term.

APPENDIX C—GLOSSARY

This section contains additional explanations for the terms used in this book rather than detailed definitions.

Asset class (Ch. 3, 6, 11, 17 and Appendix B): a group of investments with similar characteristics; the three main asset classes are stocks, bonds, and cash.

Behavioral finance (Ch. 7 and 18): a field of finance that studies an investor's psychological behavior and its influence on finance theories.

Bottom-up approach (Ch. 2): a fundamental analysis that focuses on the strength of an individual investment (bottom) and then further research into industry/sector or overall economic outlook (up); the opposite of a "top-down approach."

Breakpoint discount (Ch. 14): the discount that an investor receives on the sales charge or commission in the fund if he or she invests for or above a certain dollar amount (called the breakpoint).

Commodity Trading Adviser (CTA) (Ch. 11): a professional money manager or firm that provides advice for commodity trading, generally using a proprietary trading system.

Convertible bond (Ch. 6): a type of debt that can be converted to a specified amount of the firm's equity within a specified period of time.

Cost-benefit analysis (Ch. 10): a decision-making tool that analyzes and compares driven benefits with associated costs.

Derivative (Ch. 3, 5 and 12): a security whose value is derived from other underlying assets.

EDGAR (Ch. 13): Electronic Data Gathering, Analysis, and Retrieval system is governed by the U.S. Securities and Exchange Commission (SEC) and provides investors with information.

Front-end load mutual fund (Ch. 14): a mutual fund's sales charge or commission is charged to the investor up front at the time of purchase; the opposite of a "back-end load mutual fund."

Fund of funds (Ch. 11): a fund that invests in other funds, also known as a "multi-manager investment."

High-yield bond (Ch. 6): a bond that has a lower credit rating, thereby paying higher yields than investment-grade bonds, also known as a "junk bond"; the opposite of a "high-quality bond" (Ch. 6).

Illiquidity risk (Ch. 11 and 12): the risk of an investment being not converted to cash or redeemed at a fair market value upon an investor's request.

Impact investing (Ch. 5): "socially responsible investing" (Ch. 5) with positive screening, which means investing in socially responsible companies; negative screening means avoiding investing in the companies that are not socially responsible.

Intrinsic value (Ch. 5 and Appendix B): the fair value of an investment based on the fundamental analysis.

Life cycle (Ch. 1 and Appendix B): an investor's life cycle includes an accumulation phase, consolidation phase, and spending phase.

Load mutual fund (Ch. 14): a mutual fund with a sales charge or commission; the opposite of a "no-load mutual fund" (Ch. 11 and 14).

Managed futures (Ch. 11, 12, 13, and 14): an investment strategy or industry that involves an active sale and purchase of derivative securities, such as futures products.

Market capitalization (Ch. 6): a total market value of a publicly traded company based on the calculation of the number of shares outstanding multiplied by its share price.

Material (Ch. 5, 11, 16 and Appendix B): information that is relevant to an investor, when making an investment decision, because the information is likely to affect the value of an investment.

Money market fund (Ch. 11): a mutual fund that invests in short-term, liquid, and high-quality debt securities; as our discussion is related to retail investors, I exclude *new money-market rule* and disregard the differences among money market funds, prime funds, and government money funds. For more detail, see **Appendix D—Resources**.

Neuroeconomics (Ch. 18): a field of study that incorporates psychology and neuroscience into economics; it studies how psychological behaviors affect financial decisions and the consequences of those behaviors in order to understand how emotions play a role in economics.

Passively managed index fund (Ch. 8): a fund that replicates the performance of an underlying index (fully or partially) rather than being actively managed by a fund manager.

Preferred stock (Ch. 6 and 11): a type of stock that has characteristics of both bonds and common stocks due to a relatively fixed dividend and a higher claim on assets than common stocks.

Private equity (Ch. 12 and 13): a type of equity that is not publicly traded on a stock exchange; typically operates as funds; an investor provides capital to the company and takes an equity ownership in the company.

Proprietary fund (Ch. 14): a fund that is managed, distributed, and owned by an in-house financial institution; the opposite of "non-proprietary funds" that are managed by an outside company, which are the common funds that most investors know as mutual funds or ETFs.

Relative valuation method (Ch. 10): a valuation method that compares a company's value to the benchmark or peer group; the opposite of an "absolute valuation method."

Socially responsible investing (SRI) (Ch. 5): an investment strategy that targets not only financial returns but positive social contributions in environmental, social, and governance (ESG) categories, also known as "sustainable investing."

Technical analysis (Ch. 8 and Appendix B): an analysis method that studies price movements and trends rather than the fundamentals of the security.

Trading at a discount or premium (Ch. 10): when the current price of the security is lower (or higher) than its intrinsic value, it's considered as trading at a discount (or premium).

Unsolicited order (Ch. 2): an order that is generated by a client, not recommended by a financial professional.

APPENDIX D—RESOURCES

This section contains links to the sites that are mentioned throughout the book.

http://www.finra.org/investors (Ch. 10)

https://www.investor.gov/additional-resources/news-alerts/alerts-bulletins/investor-bulletin-accredited-investors (Ch. 11)

https://www.sec.gov/spotlight/money-market.shtml (Ch. 11)

http://www.finra.org/industry/suitability (Ch. 12)

http://www.finra.org/investors/suitability-what-investors-need-know (Ch. 12)

http://brokercheck.finra.org (Ch. 13 and 15)

https://www.sec.gov/edgar/searchedgar/webusers.htm (Ch. 13)

https://www.dol.gov/ProtectYourSavings/FactSheet.htm (Ch. 13)

https://www.cfainstitute.org/learning/future/pages/index.aspx (Ch. 15)

https://www.sec.gov/investor/brokers.htm (Ch. 15)

SMART INVESTORS CAN
CHANGE THE GAME

Many investors lose interest due to continuous disappointments. Consequently, financial professionals end up with fewer clients and less revenue. When this happens, they might focus more on selling products (instead of managing money) and accumulating new assets to make up for having fewer clients. There's a sad correlation between unhappy investors who stop investing and financial professionals' altered focus on quantity rather than the quality of service (i.e., sales rather than money management). This is a "lose-lose" situation for everyone.

But this can be changed if investors know how investing works. As an investor, if you understand the process, you'll know what to look for and feel more comfortable. And as you become savvier, you'll be able to distinguish ethical financial professionals from mere salespeople. Doing the right thing for their clients will innately provide incentives for financial professionals as well. The more professionals are focused on helping clients invest, the more likely investors will be to remain long-term investors regardless of the business cycle or market volatility.

The investment market would also react positively with an influx of currently uninvested cash. Ethical and fair investment practices can help more people accumulate wealth in a sustainable way, which would affect economic growth and build a stronger middle class with healthier retirement savings. The ripple effects, in this case, would be powerful.

www.ingramcontent.com/pod-product-compliance
Lightning Source LLC
Chambersburg PA
CBHW020837210326
41598CB00019B/1930